D0006853

From My

Kitchen Window

By

Jessie Rice Sandberg

SWORD OF THE LORD PUBLISHERS

Murfreesboro, Tennessee

Copyright 1963 by
SWORD OF THE LORD PUBLISHERS
ISBN 0-87398-261-4

Printed in U. S. A.

CONTENTS

FOREWORD

She is a distinguished, gifted Christian woman now, who writes this book. But to me, she is number four of my six beloved and unusual daughters, my girl. And of course we wouldn't let anyone else write the Foreword to this book.

Once, as a little girl playing in the yard with sisters and cousins, she lighted a small firecracker, and it exploded in her fingers. Running to Daddy, with eyes big with fright, she cried out, "Daddy, pray!" As I held her tight, prayed for the pain to stop and kissed her numb fingers, she smiled, dried her tears and said, "It's all right now, Daddy!"

In Binghamton, New York, she rode a sled down a long hill. When it overturned, her face was skinned. It was Daddy who convinced her that her looks were not permanently ruined. In a few days the scratches were gone and the face as lovely as ever.

When she had her tonsils removed, it was Daddy who stood beside the operating table and told her not to be afraid, to breathe in the ether.

Daddy officiated at her wedding to Don.

So Daddy, selfish but proud, as daddies are, writes the Foreword to her first book.

These chapters, which appeared first as a weekly column for wives and mothers in THE SWORD OF THE LORD, provoked a most enthusiastic response. Not only women, but preachers, too, write of how blessed these little talks are. When someone wrote, "The first thing I read in THE SWORD each week is FROM MY KITCHEN WINDOW, I, the editor, who likes to pretend EDITOR'S NOTES should be read first, threatened Jessie, "One more letter like that and your column is out!" I didn't mean it, of course, for I am glad that many read that charming, heart-warming column first. And you will love them, will sometimes laugh and sometimes cry, and always, I trust, be blessed as you read these little chapters of Christian comment and counsel to our beloved wives and mothers.

Mrs. Sandberg is a graduate of Wheaton College, is an artist who worked full time at the Sword of the Lord Foundation until her marriage. She has sung in the Rice Sisters Duet team for four years on the nationwide Voice of Revival Broadcast. She is a soul-winning Christian. You will see her pictured with her family opposite this Foreword, and you will meet them all on the following delightful pages.

Now with Jessie, we pray God will bless every heart that reads this book, and that the dear Lord Jesus may be made very near and dear on every page.

John R. Rice

March, 1963

Moving

I have never liked moving. In the first place, it forces me to choose between valuable possessions and less valuable ones, which is always a little heart-rending. The old love letters, the untried recipes clipped from numerous magazines, a child's first drawing of a barely-distinguishable horse--all must face the question, "Shall we save it or shall we throw it away?" Almost invariably, as I cart a box of old papers out to be burned, I feel a little pang of regret, wondering if I'll be sorry.

And then there's that feeling of attachment one always has for the old house, no matter how inadequate or antiquated it might have been. The drafty old rooms become warm and cozy in retrospect. The walls and woodwork, so often spotted by little hands, somehow take on a glow of friendly familiarity when one is about to leave them permanently. There is no triteness in the saying that "Home is where the heart is."

I remember so clearly the words Dad used in the ceremony the night Don and I were married. "Whether or not it be a bare, rented room or a palace, it is a heavenly garden, if love is there." In my mind's eye there is still a wonderful beauty in our first little apartment where we put up our first little Christmas tree, cried together over the loss of our first little baby, sang together at our little piano, laughed at our own personal little jokes; where I first learned to make Swedish meatballs, and where we proudly entertained our first company. So what if we shared a bath with two other apartments, or if our bedroom was up under attic eaves, or if our old cookstove turned the little kitchen into a furnace--we were happy beyond description. We had everything earth could offer--and Heaven beside.

Now, for the first time in our married lives we are in our really, truly "owned" home--not actually paid for yet, you know, but one where we may put up bookshelves as we like, and plant tulips along the front porch if we please. For my husband, who went from a childhood orphanage to an army barrack, to a college dormitory, our new home has been a source of wonder and joy. And even as we enjoy and thank the Lord for its comfort and beauty, there always seems to be that unseen finger of caution which warns, "This is temporary. Don't hold on too tight to that which you cannot keep forever." It's like the old love letters--you can keep the love and the happy memories, but the paper won't last forever.

We haven't had a formal "house dedication" yet, though we plan to soon. We'd like to have friends and family in and we'll no doubt serve

a little coffee and cake. Maybe my little sis, Joy, will sing, "Bless This House." And in each room we will offer prayer--that someone will be saved within our walls very soon, that the home established here will bear fruit in the lives of our children in the years to come, that visitors will find rest, comfort and fellowship, and that our own hearts will be daily refreshed and prepared for the work of the Lord. If all this is true, and please God, it will be, then we will have built with gold, silver, and precious stones.

"Except the Lord build the house, they labour in vain that build it."--Ps. 127:1.

On Being a Swede

Ever since I became Mrs. Donald E. Sandberg, I have gotten a real kick out of being a secondhand Swede. I've enjoyed watching my little blond, pink-cheeked children grow to look more and more like their tall, blond Daddy, and it has been fun to see my name added to the family tree so full of Johnsons, Swansons, and Andersons!

One of the nicest things has been inheriting Don's lovely ninety-year-old grandmother who, after fifty years in America, still prefers her beloved native tongue. I will never forget one of my earliest conversations with her. She greeted me by name, kissed me, and then rapidly began to talk to me in Swedish. "Wait a minute, there," my husband interrupted. "You know Jessie can't speak Swedish." Grandma looked startled and then said to me in English, "You can't? Well, why didn't your mother and father ever teach you?" I don't think anyone to this day has ever tried to explain that my Scotch-Irish-French-background parents couldn't teach me to speak Swedish if they wanted to.

I like the way the Swedes do things; they work hard at everything they tackle. The women are nearly always marvelous housekeepers, and their cooking is out of this world. They are sociable people and have warm, friendly ways very much like Southerners. They are artistic and creative, and their singing is usually rich and enthusiastic. I'm really pretty proud of my adopted heritage.

Another thing Swedes are strong on is tradition. My favorite of the Sandberg family traditions is the authentic smorgasbord held every Christmas Eve and served in true Swedish style. There is always Prassa sylta (pressed veal and pork), Frukt soppa (fruit soup), Swedish meatballs, potatis Korv (potato sausage, rice pudding, Swedish brown beans, pickled beets, bund ost (caraway cheese), Swedish rye bread, homemade root beer, and occasionally Lutfisk (stock fish) with mustard gravy. Since I am a junior member of the clan and especially since my experience with Scandinavian cookery is limited, I am usually asked to contribute something which requires little culinary skill--like relishes or good old American ice cream!

Well, I may never look like a Swede, cook like a Swede, or talk in a good Swedish brogue, but no one can deny the fact that I married a Swede and my name is clearly listed in the family genealogy.

Being in God's family is sort of like that, too, isn't it? We sometimes shamefully come short of proving our royal heritage by the way we talk and act and look, but when we are married into the family and our names are written in the Book of Life, no one can deny us the rights and privileges of the children of God.

A Time to Wait

We are expecting a baby at our house! Our three-and-a-half-year-old Carol says she wants a "Laurie Ann." (That is the name of a favorite baby cousin. She thinks one orders babies by brand name just like any other product--with size, shape, and color clearly specified!) Jimmy doesn't have any preferences--he just wants a "beebee." My husband teasingly tells me he thinks it really ought to be a Boxer pup since we already have one apiece of the human variety--a boy and a girl!

Of course the marvelous thing about having a baby is that whatever God sends always turns out to be what will bring the greatest joy and blessing. I read somewhere that a famous doctor said he hoped the day would never come when the sex of a child could be definitely predetermined or known. I somehow feel that is one of the mysteries of life God intends to keep locked out of our frail, human understanding. How unfortunate it would be if one could "order" a specific sex and then live to regret the decision for the rest of his life!

I always enjoy the sort of "clubby" feeling there is among pregnant women. We love to compare aches and pains (or lack of them), doctors, previous pregnancies, weight, preferences in names, sex, hospitals and the dozens of other things related to having a baby. Perhaps there is no other experience common to women which is quite so uniting as this. The physical processes and emotional needs of a woman expecting a baby do not have a great deal to do with race, economic situation, location, or even especially with age. Giving birth is all at once both the most common and still the most unique of all human experiences.

I wonder if there is any period of time which seems quite as long as that nine months before a baby is born. In her little poem, "Thoughts of an Expectant Mother," Ellen Ferraro Thompson says:

"God gives us a time to wait--
A curse and blessing both.
Time to knit for some;
Time to pray for some;
Time to read for some;
And a time to think, for all--...."

I am almost certain that God arranged the length of time necessary to having a baby for reasons even more important than the child's physical development. Even as the progressing months of pregnancy require a certain slowing down physically, there also seems to develop a certain need for taking stock of oneself mentally and spiritually. Surely, no woman, except for some deliberate and extreme perversion of heart and mind, could be an atheist after the experience of childbirth. There seems to be a special sense in which the marvel and certainty of creation is unique in the expectation and birth of a baby.

Isn't it wonderful that the Lord sometimes puts us in situations where we have to wait? Here is one area of life which cannot be affected by all the time-study plans and accelerated production methods of modern industry! No matter how busy or impatient we are, God gives us--a time to wait.

There are so many blessings to be learned in having to wait. One young woman I know who went through school days and into an early marriage completely absorbed in being pretty and popular and having a good time, told me

11

that in all her life she had never taken the time to consider her need for a Saviour and salvation, though she had been witnessed to often, until she was expecting her first baby. Then, she said, she was almost overwhelmed with a sense of responsibility for the immortal soul being created. Of course it was not difficult then for a godly relative to lead her to the Lord.

In the last weeks of pregnancy when the days seem especially long and the body especially weary, I always take special delight in reading over and over again Psalm 37. Much of the Bible gives instructions for action and warfare, but this chapter is just full of wonderful passive commands such as "Trust in the Lord," "Delight thyself also in the Lord," "Rest in the Lord," "Wait on the Lord," "Fret not thyself . . . ," "Commit thy way unto the Lord. . . ." And then while you are resting, be sure to read that sweet passage from Isaiah 40 (verse 11):

"He shall feed his flock like a shepherd; he shall gather the lambs with his arm, and carry them in his bosom, and shall gently lead those that are with young."

How wonderful to have "a time to wait. . ."!

Pants Like Daddy's

Our little Jimmy has a new pair of pants! Not the baby-coverall kind with snap-shut legs and crossed straps in back. These are real, grown-up trousers, complete with belt, zipper and creases down the front of the legs. The fact that the pants will barely stay in place around his fat little tummy doesn't disturb Jimmy one bit. He hitches them up with both hands and says proudly, "Daddy's pants."

Jimmy's emulation of his daddy doesn't end with the pants. He tries to walk like his daddy, lead the singing like he sees his daddy do it, and to the fullest extent of his baby-ability he is trying to be just like his daddy. The results are always interesting, usually hilarious, and sometimes shocking.

Did you ever stop to think what particular people had the greatest influence in your life? Some, perhaps, you secretly determined to be like in looks or manner or dress. Others, by training and example, helped to mold your character, inspire your ambitions. A few, by prayers and tears, helped to determine your spiritual destiny.

Of all the people who had some influence in creating my own tastes and interests and personality, some I remember with special fondness--a third-grade art teacher who made me think I could be an artist if I REALLY wanted to; a marvelous, talented lady with five boys for whom I did housework as a high school girl; a favorite uncle, big and handsome, who made even the simplest pleasures as exciting as a circus; dear Miss Fairy, expert at making fudge and popcorn balls and at mending broken hearts; Mrs. Mandy, a piano teacher who always wore lily-of-the-valley perfume; a young people's director, a college friend, a lady doctor, a colonel's wife, a young negro girl, and, of course, my own mother and father who without question held the greatest influence in my life.

Influence is a strange, subtile thing. It rarely announces its presence with a brass band. The people with whom you mingle day by day, the things you read and see and hear--all of these make up the person who is you.

A young preacher I know who was born and reared in the Northwest preaches in a way that would make you think he had never been north of the Mason-Dixon line. The fact is, he got most of his human inspiration for preaching from a greatly blessed southern preacher whom he admires tremendously. He has watched and listened to the great preacher from the South until his own vocal inflections, gestures and vocabulary have a distinctly southern flavor. In an effort to be like his idol in blessing and usefulness, the young preacher has subconsciously acquired his outward characteristics as well. Actually, of course, this is a good thing rather than bad. It is always a blessing for young people to be exposed to and influenced by men and women who are doing things for God.

Paul said, "Be ye followers of me...," and in a sense all of us are saying that to our children, our Sunday School classes and to other young people around us--just by being what we are. It is not an accident that little children want to be like their parents. It is a gift as precious as sight and hearing--arranged by God to make discipline effective and to make

13

child-rearing a joyful and rewarding responsibility.

Occasionally one hears a mother say, "Well, my daughter won't listen to me. After all, I'm just her mother!" And the sad truth is that a mother who does not prayerfully use the marvelous gift of influence while her children are small, will in all certainty lose it when those children become teen-agers.

Most of us, as women, will never sway the world with great political speeches or great deeds of humanitarianism. We will never preach the sermons that will bring thousands to the Saviour. In fact, most of us will never be known beyond that small circle of family, friends and acquaintances which touch the span of an average lifetime. But we could, with God's blessing, influence the boy or girl who will become a D. L. Moody, a Queen Esther, a David Livingstone, or a John Wesley. Perhaps my own son or daughter...that wistful little girl in my Sunday School class...that boy who mows my lawn and who probably doesn't even remember my name--I wonder... what are they learning from me?

Boys

I grew up in a family of girls, so I am constantly surprised by the antics of little boys.

Our Jimmy is just eighteen months old and already he is showing every indication that he is a boy--all boy. Teasing his big sister is already his favorite pastime and he has a special affinity for dirt. He loves trucks, dogs, hammers and anything which makes noise or has a moving part, and his daddy is absolutely the be-and-end-all!

Do you have a boy at your house? If you do, you will enjoy the following excerpts from Alan Beck's delightful essay called, "What Is a Boy?"

"...Boys are found everywhere--on top of, underneath, inside of, climbing on, swinging from, running around, or jumping to. Mothers love them, little girls hate them, older sisters and brothers tolerate them, adults ignore them, and Heaven protects them.

"A boy is Truth with dirt on its face, Beauty with a cut on its finger, Wisdom with bubble gum in its hair, and the Hope of the future with a frog in its pocket.

"A boy is a composite. He has the appetite of a horse, the digestion of a sword swallower, the energy of a pocket-size atomic bomb, the curiosity of a cat, the lungs of a dictator, the imagination of a Paul Bunyan, the shyness of a violet, the audacity of a steel trap, the enthusiasm of a firecracker, and when he makes something he has five thumbs on each hand.

"...Nobody else is so early to rise, or so late to supper. Nobody else gets so much fun out of trees, dogs, and breezes. Nobody else can cram into one pocket a rusty knife, a half-eaten apple, three feet of string, ...2 gum drops, 6 cents, a sling shot, a chunk of unknown substance, and a genuine supersonic code ring with a secret compartment.

"A boy is a magical creature. You can lock him out of your work shop, but you can't lock him out of your heart. You can get him out of your study, but you can't get him out of your mind. Might as well give up--he is your captor, your jailer--a freckle-faced, pint-size, cat-chasing bundle of noise. But when you come home at night with only the shattered pieces of your hopes and dreams, he can mend them like new with two magic words--"Hi, Dad!"

What a wonderful thing it is to have a boy--a future president, perhaps, a great preacher or missionary, some great man who will help to mold the course of history! Every parent cherishes some secret hope or dream for the future of his offspring. But how frightening to realize the potential for heartache and trouble in a son without godly training or prayerful discipline...

This week there will be a trial in our county courthouse--a sobering one for every man or woman who has a boy. Twelve boys--members of a teen-age crime ring (the youngest being 13 years of age) will be tried for an astounding list of crimes--everything from simple vandalism to car theft and burglary. The sad part of the story is that the boys do not come from the slums of Chicago but from our beautiful and well-heeled sister-village of Glen Ellyn. Even sadder is the report from the judge that some of the parents showed shocking unconcern over their sons' difficulties during the preliminary hearings. One father even fell asleep while the charges against his son were being read. Another father had never bothered to question the basement full of loot his son

had been collecting over a period of six weeks.

Did the parents become failures with the first set of stolen car keys, the first broken windowpane? Of course not! But the hard part is facing the fact that the winsome six-year-old with the toothless grin, the cherub-faced three-year-old, and even my lisping, toddling, precious Jimmy--all of them, without earnest, prayerful, day-by-day training, are potential criminals. Does it frighten you? It certainly does me!

Please read these Scriptures:

"He that spareth his rod hateth his son: but he that loveth him chasteneth him betimes." --Prov. 13:24.

"Train up a child in the way he should go: and when he is old, he will not depart from it." --Prov. 22:6.

"Chasten thy son while there is hope, and let not thy soul spare for his crying." --Prov. 19:18.

"Foolishness is bound in the heart of a child; but the rod of correction shall drive it far from him." --Prov. 22:15.

The Blessings of Trouble

We were having our family devotions at the breakfast table this morning just as we always do. Three-year-old Carol was praying and as usual her prayer was getting long and full of childish prattle, so my mind began to wander. Would the car start? Should I try to get the ironing done or finish making my husband's pajamas? I mustn't forget to call Joanna and find out how the new baby is getting along.... Suddenly I began to be aware again of the prayer. "...and bless all the troubles we got. Amen." I heard Don snicker and then try to cover it up with a cough. Later, when he was gone and the children were busy playing, I laughed to myself, right out loud. "Bless all the troubles we got...." What does a three-year-old know about trouble!

You know, trouble is a strange thing. It arrives in dark robes of despair and uncertainty, and not until it is already behind us do we recognize that our unwelcome intruder has been God's love and mercy in disguise. How often the Lord uses difficulty to give us "the best" in place of "the good."

Somewhere I heard (and I do wish I could remember the source) that "it is better to be

17

in the dark and feel God's hand than to be in the light and have Him far away."

The sweetest memories I have are centered around the time of one of my deepest disappointments. Christmas in our family has always been wonderful, but the holiday season of 1954 promised to be the best ever. Don and I had been married not quite a year and we were happily looking forward to the prospect of a baby due the middle of February. We already had a crib and some pretty little soft things suitable for either a boy or girl. In our expectancy, the story of Jesus' birth held special sweetness and we felt our cup of joy was truly running over.

Unexpectedly, however, just two days before Christmas our baby was born, and died within the hour. Besides the sorrow of losing a little one, we had to face the knowledge that our child had had some grotesque and heartbreaking deformities. It is difficult to describe the sense of shock and feeling of inadequacy which we felt. Of course there were tears and the nagging question, "Why? Why? Why?"

The Lord in His mercy did not leave us in despair long. We learned immediately how

kind people could be and how eager they were to help bear our sorrow. That in itself was rich recompense. And what a tenderness and sweetness was added to our marriage and home in the sharing of that common grief! The meaning of Christmas itself was so much more real and Heaven so much more dear. Perhaps the greatest blessing of all has been the wonder and realization of what a privilege it is to have the little children which the Lord has since added to our home. Do you think I would ask now that anything about that experience be changed? Of course not!

My dad's favorite hymn, and I think perhaps mine, too, is "How Firm a Foundation" by George Keith, with the words taken almost directly from Isaiah 41:10 and 43:2. Here is the message:

"How firm a foundation, ye saints of the Lord,
Is laid for your faith in His excellent Word!
What more can He say than to you He hath said,
To you, who for refuge to Jesus have fled?

"Fear not, I am with thee, O be not dismayed,
For I am thy God, I will still give thee aid;

I'll strengthen thee, help thee, and cause thee to stand,

Upheld by My gracious, omnipotent hand.

"When through the deep waters I call thee to go,
The rivers of sorrow shall not overflow;
For I will be with thee thy trials to bless,
And sanctify to thee thy deepest distress.

"When through fiery trials thy pathway shall lie,
My grace, all-sufficient, shall be thy supply;
The flames shall not hurt thee, I only design
Thy dross to consume, and thy gold to refine."

Yes, Lord--please do--"bless all the troubles we got." And sanctify to us our deepest distress.

Rainy Days

Even before I opened my eyes this morning I knew it was raining. There's a kind of snug, warm feeling to a bed on a rainy morning-- maybe it's the monotonous patter of the drops on the roof, or maybe just the dullness of the morning light coming through the window--I'm not sure. Whatever causes it, there is just a certain sort of "feel" to a rainy day.

I always like to clean drawers on a wet day. Maybe your drawers don't get like mine. My husband is one of those orderly people who puts certain things in certain positions in certain drawers and then they just stay that way. Not so with me. If a button comes off Jimmy's coat in the living room, I'm likely to put it in the top desk drawer--just until I can get a needle and thread, of course--and it stays right there with the little screws off things, the single lost shoestring, the recipe for chop suey I was looking for yesterday, and the letter to Aunt Minner which I meant to answer last week.

You can see what cleaning that drawer involves. The button must be sewed on Jimmy's coat which only serves to remind me of the hem which is coming out on one of Carol's dresses; the lost shoestring must be matched up with its partner which reminds me that all the shoes need polishing; the little screws must be put back in where they fell out which only reminds me that immumerable screws all over the house really ought to be tightened; the rec- ipe for chop suey should be filed and that re- minds me that I should copy that recipe I pro- mised Mom; the letter to Aunt Minner must be answered and, by the way, I really ought to get off a birthday card to Uncle Ray! Well, I don't need to tell you that one drawer can mean a whole day's work what with all that chain reac- tion!

I was just thinking that prayer is sort of like that. We plead, "Lord, I can't find the answer to this or that problem." Perhaps it's money problems--or wayward children--or a need for strength or peace, or contentment. And some- how in the process of looking, and praying and searching and sorting through all the broken, undone things in our hearts, the Lord seems to say, "Well, get this thing fixed and out of the

way, and you will find it," or "Just put these interests and desires in their proper place and you will see what you are looking for." Then, each matter brought to the Lord in confession helps to remind us of other hidden, forgotten sins.

Just this morning I read D. L. Moody's won- derful sermon on Confession (from the October 30, 1959, SWORD OF THE LORD). I was so im- pressed by a quotation of Richard Sibbes I want to repeat it here:

"This is the way to give glory to God; when we have laid open our souls to God and laid as much against ourselves as the Devil could do that way . . . The more we accuse and judge ourselves, and set up a tribunal in our hearts, certainly there will follow an incredible ease."

Maybe that's why God sends the rainy days. Do your desk drawers need cleaning? And what about your heart?

"Search me, O God, and know my heart: try me, and know my thoughts: And see if there be any wicked way in me, and lead me in the way everlasting."

A Country Store

Not far from where we live there is a little old-fashioned country store. I'm sure it has been there for years. All around it the rich Illinois farmland has been subdivided into half-acre lots and so it is rapidly being surrounded by modern new homes--split level, ranch and Cape Cod.

The proprietress of the store is a little old lady who was born on the old family homestead which once covered this whole area. Just the other day she told me with a bit of nostalgia that our house sits right in the middle of the old turnip patch which was her specific responsibility as a little farm girl. (Incidentally, she didn't have to prove it to me about the turnips --we picked turnip greens out of the front yard half the summer!)

But back to the store. It is old and musty and it is stocked mainly with assorted canned goods, a few staples--flour, cereal, sugar--and of course the usual assortment of ballpoint pens, novelty salt-and-pepper shakers, and penny

"God give us women. These times are sore,
  No woman ever faced the likes before.
Women we need with wealth of mind and gifted,
Women who will not swerve nor shirk their
  task.
Women with hearts to Heaven uplifted,
  Women with faith a vaster good to ask.
Brave women, this is no time to falter
  Who dares be vainly weak or idly gay,
When placed upon the nation's altar.
'Tis women's noblest, best, God wants today.
Spurn, then, to live in ease or pleasure;
  Justice would have your richest treasure,
A woman like Deborah in Holy Writ,
  Be glad in peace or war to do your bit!"

                                    Anon.

candy. It is the meeting place for the school children every afternoon and the old-timers still drop in occasionally to gossip a little and pass the time of day. The rest of the neighborhood frequents the store spasmodically--usually for an emergency loaf of bread or quart of milk.

The store seems to have no regular hours; if the little neon light in the front window is on, then the store is open. It may be open Sunday afternoon or closed on Tuesday morning depending on the whims or the activities of the little lady in charge. No one complains--there are no special sales or bargains anyway. We patronize the store when convenient and the proprietress accepts our business when it is convenient to her.

All in all, one wonders how the little business can survive--and I dare say survive is all it really does!

One day last week as my husband and I were driving by, we noticed that the store was closed (as it had been for several days) and that several cars were parked around the little building. We speculated as to what might be the reason: perhaps there were visiting relatives,

or maybe the old lady was very sick. It could have been for some very important reason or for no reason at all.

Afterwards I got to thinking how often our service for the Lord is like that little country store. We are in business all right--most of the time--provided it is convenient--if the circumstances are right--if we are in the mood--if there isn't something more important, etc., etc. Occasionally we sell a little "canned" gospel--a tract hurriedly and embarrassingly shoved under someone's nose, or left under the plate for the waitress, along with a 10¢ tip. We are forever giving people worn-out, musty old testimonies of God's grace ten years ago. How rarely do we offer anything so fresh and Spirit-filled that people are compelled to "buy."

The truth is that most of us are not really trying to sell anything. We are pleasant, unobnoxious, ease-loving Christians who make a pretense of giving service; we actually do not even care that poor lost sinners desperately need what we have to offer. We are sitting behind our little shabby store-fronts of Christianity with stock too meager, too shopworn, or too old to make much of an impression on those who need our wares.

Jesus has said, "I am the bread of life: he that cometh to me shall never hunger; and he that believeth on me shall never thirst." Do you have any fresh bread for those in need?

Resolutions for Wives

The other day I was going through a box of old books and papers when I happened to run into the little notebook I had kept of our wedding plans. I had forgotten what loving, careful attention a bride-to-be gives to each little detail of that one big day. There was a diagram of the church, a list of friends to whom invitations would be sent, a list of the music to be used, a wonderful recipe for "Groom's Cake" and a check list for things to be done the day of the wedding. Also included was a list of resolutions I had almost forgotten--written late one night just a day or two before the wedding. As I read them again six years later, I couldn't help wondering what my husband would think about how well the resolutions were or were not carried out. Shall I list them just as they were written--as a prayer?

1. Let my home be a place of rest--a citadel for my husband--where he can freely express his opinions, share his confidences or find perfect quiet if he wishes it.

2. Let it be orderly and clean--but let clean-liness and beauty never be the end in itself--only the oil which keeps the home relationships running smoothly, the key to relaxation for tired bodies; a pleasant atmosphere to share with friends.

3. Let me be responsive to his needs--joy-ful always, enthusiastic about his plans, under-standing when he is discouraged, patient when he seems unreasonable. Let my criticism be scarce, brief and kind.

4. Let me be as concerned about my per-sonal appearance now as I was when we first met. Let me keep my person and possessions neat and in order.

5. Let me never lose my zest for living. Help me to be interested in others and in the world around me, not forgetting to feed my mind and train my hands so that I will be in-teresting to be with and well-informed.

6. Give me ingenuity and skill in making things do when times are hard and finances are low. Let me be content with the things I am able to possess; let me never hinge my happi-ness on "belongings."

7. Let me be free of jealousy and suspicion; not demanding all his time and attention. Let me never hold a grudge in my heart so that it becomes a root of bitterness. Let caresses and tender words never lose their sweetness and let love be sufficient reward for any deed of kindness.

8. Let me always hold him in a place of es-teem--privately and before others. May I re-member to check any word of belittlement or sarcasm. Help me to keep his private affairs in strict confidence.

9. May I always be an influence for good--encouraging him to do right whatever the price; helping him to put the Lord before myself.

*　　　　*　　　　*

After the everyday wear and little domestic crises of several years of marriage, those resolutions seem a little idealistic, but at least the principles are still right. Maybe I'd bet-ter paste them over my kitchen sink. It's so easy to forget what a shining example of a wife I was planning to be!

The Bible sets some pretty high standards for wives in both the Old Testament and the New. Sometime, when you really feel a need for a little soul-searching in your role as wife and mother, read Proverbs 31 and Ephesians 5. It is pretty revealing.

*

*

*

I Love You

The year I was engaged to be married and was walking around in that state of starry-eyed confusion peculiar only to brides, my dad once laughingly said to me, "Jessie, I don't think you fell in love; you just climbed in!" At the time, I considered that remark an insult. Now, after a few years of real married bliss I know that dad was not only right, but that the idea is not such a bad one after all!

Do you remember how you fell in love? With Don, my first impression was that he was fun to be with and that other people liked him. My second was that he had some strong convictions and wasn't afraid to state them. (How well I remember thinking after one hearty discussion, "Why, he sounds just like my dad!") Third, or maybe it was fourth or fifth--who knows in what order the impressions followed --I was aware of the way he dressed, his ambitions for serving the Lord, his respect for women in general, his thoughtfulness, his enthusiasm, his family pride and a hundred other characteristics.

Those impressions, first being watered by casual conversations and then satisfying friendship, soon blossomed into a full-blown love affair! Of course I never said to myself, "I will now proceed to fall in love," but at the same time one can never say that love which has grown from hours spent together, from interests, hopes and dreams shared--is an accidental thing. Love, the real honest-to-goodness kind, is something which is deliberately nurtured and tended with care. It does not just "happen."

David the psalmist said, "I will love the Lord, my God." Isn't it strange to realize that love really is primarily a matter of the will? And even after love has been felt and declared--toward the Lord, family, friends, the world--it has to be cultivated and encouraged to be a satisfying thing.

When I was growing up, our family had a little ritual which took place at least once a day, usually at mealtime. Daddy would go around the family circle and ask each one in turn, "Whose girl are you?" The standard answer, often given with a kiss, was, "Daddy's girl!" Mother and daughters alike were included in

the little ceremony. I suppose the custom seemed foolish to the occasional outsider but it was a rich and happy experience for us.

We have a similar little game with our children. Don or I will ask one of the little ones, "Who do you love?" (So what if the grammar is bad?) Then, except for those occasions when impish Jimmy wants to tease his mother by answering, "Flicka!" (that's Grandpa's dog) the answer is always "Daddy," and then "Mommy." Somehow, we never get tired of hearing those sweet, lisping words.

A famous woman writer once said, "I not only want to be loved; I want to be told that I am loved." Child psychologists say that by actual experiment they have found that tiny babies who are given expert care from the standpoint of food and clothing but who are deprived of normal expressions of love such as fondling, holding, smiles and gentle talk, fail to develop normally both physically and socially. Yet, how often we adults bury our affections for those around us deep in our heart without ever a tender expression of love or a caress.

I think it follows a logical pattern, too, to say that people who learn to express themselves easily usually do not have as difficult a time learning to say, "I'm sorry; I was wrong," or, more important, "I am a sinner. I need a Saviour."

How hungry the Saviour's heart must have been for an expression of tenderness when He said to Peter, "Lovest thou me?" and earlier when He seemed to encourage John to lay his head upon His breast. Jesus' heart seemed to crave every gesture or expression of love. Remember the instance of the children who came to Jesus and were turned away by the disciples; the case of the woman who kissed the feet of Jesus and washed His feet with her tears; and Mary who sat constantly at the feet of Jesus and was rebuked by her sister, Martha? In each instance someone thought Jesus would consider the attention and affection a nuisance or impropriety so that He nearly always had to say, "Leave them alone. Let them come to me." How sad that He who is Love should find our hearts so cold and unresponsive that we actually try to discourage the tender, spontaneous outpourings of affection that are the natural expression of real heart-love.

No wonder our poor hearts backslide so easily and so often; we neglect that most blessed task--nourishing our love for the Lord by daily expression.

How long has it been since you said, "I love you"?

Spicy Christians

I wonder if spices and seasonings fascinate you as much as they do me. Rosemary, basil, oregano, cinnamon, sage, cloves--even the names stir up all sorts of mental pictures of exotic places, interesting foods and memorable occasions. Sage sounds like a Texas prairie; rosemary reminds me of a country garden, and cinnamon brings visions of my mother's kitchen on a frosty winter morning. One of my favorite smells as a child was that of vanilla extract being fragrantly stirred into cake batter. How shocked and disappointed I was when I tasted it right from the bottle and found it to be unbearably bitter!

I've always been a little envious of my sister Grace who has a real flare for cooking with spices. She makes a wonderful golden rice dish with saffron which is very different and very delicious, and her green salads often include some herb or seasoning which is unique and interesting.

I suppose the biggest difference between a

good cook and a mediocre one is that ability to blend just the right amount and kind of seasoning with common, wholesome, properly cooked foods. Lovely, artistic salads and desserts are always fun to prepare and beautiful to behold, but almost any man will tell you that when it comes right down to being good and hungry, nothing beats a steaming pot roast with browned potatoes, carrots, and onions simmering in the gravy--all seasoned to perfection.

The commonest of all seasonings and the most essential are, of course, just plain sugar and salt. Here in America both are so available that we often forget how essential they really are, both for our pleasure in eating and our nutrition as well. Anyone who has ever had to do without one or the other for medical or economic reasons can tell you how precious their substance is. You know how the tiniest bit of sugar can improve the flavor of almost any food--green vegetables, salad dressings, meats--and salt has long been recognized as a necessary additive to almost every kind of diet all over the world. Can you imagine how flavorless foods would be if we had no sugar or salt?

It isn't any wonder, then, that the Bible had so much to say about salt. Just as food is flat and tasteless without a bit of salt, so this old world is meaningless if Christians do not provide the seasoning of the Holy Spirit's blessing and power of conviction. Unfortunately, most of us are afraid of being "salty" Christians. We enjoy being "salt" as long as it makes us more palatable to other people. On the other hand, salt brings a sting as it comes in contact with the canker sore of sin, and we cringe at the responsibility of exposing and rebuking sin. We would so much rather be wintergreen or oil of cloves--pleasant-tasting and soothing.

One interesting characteristic which salt and sugar have in common is their power to preserve foods--a quality which is especially valuable in areas where there is not good refrigeration such as most of us enjoy. How sad that the Lord intends us to be the preservative of the earth, and in mercy spares judgment, waiting for us to have still another opportunity to win those we ought to be leading to the Saviour (read II Peter 3:9). But most of us are like salt without any savor, sugar without any sweetness. We have no special influence or power for either good or evil. We don't especially help anyone, but on the other hand we don't particularly make anyone mad either.

How hungry the world is for a little pinch of salt, a little taste of the sweetness of salvation! Are you a spicy Christian?

"Ye are the salt of the earth: but if the salt have lost his savour, wherewith shall it be salted? it is thenceforth good for nothing, but to be cast out, and to be trodden under foot of men." -Matt. 5:13.

"I Wanted to Be Somebody"

Not long ago I read a condensation of Althea Gibson's book, I Wanted to Be Somebody. Miss Gibson, as you may know, is a young Negro girl who rose from a juvenile delinquent background in the slums of New York to become the Women's Tennis Champion of the World, and in the book she tells of her struggles with life and society to reach that point of fame. She closes her book by saying, "I think I've found what I want. I hope it makes me happy."

The closing comment seemed so wistful and so characteristic of all mankind that it haunted me for days. In every human heart there surely must be that craving to "be somebody." Of course the definition of the term "being somebody" would vary with almost every individual but at least we would all describe it as achieving some measure of attainment or recognition. A schoolboy wants to be like some athletic hero; a new bride hopes to win praise as an outstanding cook; a young man starting in business pictures himself as a future president of the company. All of us have secret yearnings for the things we would like to do or become in the span of a lifetime.

Even in the job of housekeeping, I occasionally find myself feeling envious of my sister-in-law Alice whose home seems to be eternally spotlessly clean, or I wish inwardly that I were famous for some special gift in cooking like my Aunt Fannie who makes absolutely mouthwatering lemon meringue pies! And then when I meet those mothers whose children always look clean and always seem well-behaved in public, I think, "Now if I were that kind of mother I would really feel like I was 'somebody.'"

Occasionally my personal dreams extend beyond the sphere of home and children. I think of what a thrill it would be to be able to stir and bless the hearts of thousands through song, or through writing or teaching, or even perhaps in painting some great and lovely picture.

Ambition--the right kind--is a wonderful thing. It is perhaps the one thing that makes hard work worthwhile, poverty bearable, starting over possible, and learning a joy. Without some measure of ambition, some sort of goal, life would be, even for a Christian, merely a series of minutes and hours and days strung together without any reason for being. Just imagine a day when you have no goals, no plans, nothing to look forward to, no work to do. Can you think of any existence more unbearable?

On the other hand, maybe it is a good thing we cannot really see our own hearts or understand fully how much of our ambition is made up of self-exploitation and our own selfish pride. So much of our work for the Lord even is done for recompense of some kind or another, whether it be recognition, prestige, material advantages, and sometimes as a form of "keeping up with the Joneses." In these days there is a certain respectability even for those who aren't Christians, in giving a little of one's time and effort and money to church work.

I think maybe the problem is that our definition of "being somebody" is not quite God's definition. Daniel 12:3 says, "They that be wise shall shine as the brightness of the firmament; and they that turn many to righteousness as the stars for ever and ever." Isn't it a strange thing that some of the people who had the great-

31

est spiritual influence on the world were by all human standards failures? John the Baptist experienced unusual fame for awhile, but then, according to his own prediction, "I must decrease, but he (Jesus) must increase." He died a martyr's death in prison, practically forgotten and unmourned. Paul, who was once proclaimed a god, later said, "I am become as the offscouring of the earth."

Maybe we need some new goals and ambitions to really become "somebody." We get so busy with our necessary but inadequate human dreams that we forget that we may become "stars" by following God's formula--leading many to righteousness.

Do you really want to "be somebody"?

Teaching Children to Memorize

We had a wonderful family pastime when I was a child which I think is almost unheard of in these days when families are so preoccupied with television and many other activities outside the home. We memorized all kinds of literature--mostly Scripture, of course, but occasionally some portions of great classical writings, sometimes little poems to help with character building, and sometimes readings which we memorized just for the fun of the learning.

It was always a part of our regular Christmas festivities to quote together the first 20 verses of Luke 2 as we sat around the lighted tree on Christmas Eve. I remember that we learned together the 28th chapter of Matthew as we drove along in the car on the way to Grandpa's house for the Easter holidays and always afterward we would quote it together at the breakfast table on Easter morning. On another occasion we learned the first few verses of John 14, besides many many individual Scriptures at different times.

Dad and Mother both loved the writings of Browning, Tennyson, and Shakespeare and so we soon became familiar with many short quotations from their writings. Two that I remember from Shakespeare at the moment are:

"How sharper than a serpent's tooth it is
To have a thankless child...."

and

"Her voice was ever soft,
Gentle, and low, an excellent
thing in woman."

And then we had a great deal of fun with James Whitcomb Riley's "Little Orphant Annie." We would quote it with all sorts of elaborate gestures, especially when we came to the closing lines:

"An' little Orphant Annie says
when the blaze is blue,
An' the lamp-wick sputters, an'
the wind goes WOO-OO!
An' you hear the crickets quit, an'
the moon is gray,
An' the lightnin'-bugs in dew is all
squenched away, --
You better mind yer parunts an'
yer teachers fond and dear,
An' churish them 'at loves you,
an' dry the orphant's tear,
An' he'p the pore an' needy ones
'at clusters all about,
Er the Gobble-uns'll git you
Ef You
Don't
Watch
Out!"

Just the other day I was amazed and pleased when a reader brought to mind two other little verses I had learned as a child, one of which I had almost forgotten.

I immediately decided to make sure that my own children learn both of them. I think they are very old and probably quite commonly known, but just in case you are not familiar with them, here they are:

"Hearts, like doors, will ope with ease
To very, very little keys,
And just remember, two of these
Are 'Thank you, Sir,' and 'If you please.'"

Whenever I was nervous or worried as a little girl, I found this next poem a great comfort:

"Said the Robin to the Sparrow:
'I should really like to know
Why these anxious human beings
Rush about and worry so?'"

"Said the Sparrow to the Robin,
'Friend, I think that it must be
That they have no Heavenly Father
Such as cares for you and me.'"

The marvelous part about learning little poems, songs, and especially Scripture verses is that they have a way of embedding themselves into one's heart and mind as in a reservoir and then presenting themselves just when needed. Just the other day our three-and-a-half-year-old Carol came running to me and

said, "Mommy, the Bible says, 'Be kind to one another' and Jimmy isn't being kind to me!" Her application of the Scripture was a little misplaced, but she had the principle right anyway.

I have very little patience with Christian educators who insist that a child should never be taught a verse or principle he does not understand. Any sensible mother teaches a child many rules and principles before the child can possibly understand the whys and wherefores of them. We do not wait until a child understands that a car may kill him before we teach him to stay out of the street. Neither should we wait until a child knows a complete system of theology before we teach him that "the wages of sin is death."

The minds of children have unlimited capacity. If we do not fill them with the things that will mold their characters and their eternal destinies, someone else will. What a privilege it is to give our children that wonderful heritage—a rich store of spiritual and sacred wisdom to bring a lifetime of blessing!

A Baby Is Born

Somewhere in the distance I heard the doctor's cheerful voice saying, "Well, you have a nice big baby boy--at least he looks mighty big. We haven't weighed him yet." A few minutes later my husband was standing at my side holding my hand and then that wonderful, indescribable sense of peace swept over me. The pain was over; the waiting was over; the months of dreaming and planning had reached fulfillment. Little Don Robert had arrived safely (all 8 lbs. 10 oz. of him!) and all was well. How happy have been these days of rest and recuperation and getting acquainted with our new little son!

The hospital in which Little Don was born is a lovely place, but quite small. All the rooms are on one floor and face out toward beautiful parks and gardens. One night shortly before I came home, three new patients were admitted to the maternity ward and it seemed likely that all three would have their babies at just about the same time. The problem lay in the fact that the hospital contained only one delivery room and one labor room, and also in the fact that all three women had the same doctor! The nurses hastily put one patient in the delivery room, one in the labor room, and the third, a seventeen-year-old girl, was placed in the room with me.

My heart was touched by my new roommate the moment I saw her. In the first place, she looked hardly old enough to be through with dolls, and she was so frightened she was shaking. She said to me, almost pitifully, "I've never been in a hospital before except to have my tonsils out and I don't think I'm going to like this." Later, as she screamed, partly from fear and partly in pain, her young husband (probably not more than eighteen himself) tried so hard to comfort her and at the same time reminded her that she must not carry on because she was disturbing the other patients on the floor. The look of seriousness and concern he wore seemed strangely out of place on his young face.

Within a few hours the baby had arrived (and in the delivery room, too!); the new mother was wheeled back into our room and was united with her proud young husband. The change was startling and complete. A frightened little girl had become a confident and happy woman. Later, she turned to me and said with an apologetic smile, "I'm sorry I made so much noise last night. You know, I thought I couldn't stand it at the time, but now as I look back, it doesn't seem like it was half bad." I thought again of Jesus' words in John 16:21 and their application in verse 22:

"A woman when she is in travail hath sorrow, because her hour is come: but as soon as she is delivered of the child, she remembereth no more the anguish, for joy that a man is born into the world.

"And ye now therefore have sorrow: but I will see you again, and your heart shall rejoice, and your joy no man taketh from you."

Did you ever stop to think how many good things come out of pain? Life at its richest and fullest is a bittersweet experience. When things come to us too easily, then the challenge of hard work is gone. If there is never any disappointment and defeat, then victory is not quite so sweet. If we are never snubbed and

ignored, then we cannot fully taste the joy of tenderness and kindness. And so the beauty and wonder of a new little baby is much greater because we have waited and felt pain and paid the price of giving birth..

How interesting that the Apostle John should compare the joy that follows the birth of a new baby to the joy of seeing the Lord Jesus when He comes again! Do your sorrows and problems seem almost more than you can stand? Then rest again in Jesus' wonderful promise:

"And ye now therefore have sorrow: but I will see you again, and your heart shall rejoice, and your joy no man taketh from you."

Something for Nothing

I love this time of year! For some reason autumn always makes me feel younger than does the springtime. Maybe it's because I associate the fall with school days and all the related activities--football games, bonfires, walks through crisp brown leaves, and holidays enjoyed only by young people--like Halloween.

Halloween was a day we always looked forward to because it was an excuse for a party and for dressing up. Of course we were taught not to put any stock in the superstitions of the day, nor were we allowed to take part in any Halloween pranks, but we did have lots of fun bobbing for apples, eating popcorn balls and dressing in all kinds of odd outfits. Our costumes were not the kind bought at the store for $5.98. We made them up from anything we could salvage from the attic, the basement, or the garage. The results were sometimes ingenious, often weird, and always funny. Sometimes we planned "spook houses" which were

definitely more foolish than frightening, even though they always included what we hoped would appear to be eerie lights and blood-curdling shrieks! Unfortunately, the laughter usually ruined any illusion of "spookiness" we might have hoped to achieve.

We were never allowed to take part in the practice of playing "Trick or Treat." If you have children, I'm sure you are familiar with the game. It consists of ringing a doorbell and then yelling, "Trick or treat!" The idea is, supposedly, that if the occupants of the house do not provide a treat such as candy, apples or cookies, then some kind of prank will be played--garbage can overturned, windows soaped, etc. In our neighborhood the Trick or Treating is done generally by smaller children, and I think there is usually no intention of playing any pranks. Still, I wonder it it doesn't give an early introduction to our national obsession --trying to get something for nothing.

Did you ever stop to realize how many influences in our modern society help to make our children feel they are being cheated unless they can get something for nothing? Most of them are things which in themselves are nei-

37

ther illegal nor immoral but they contribute to the general impression that it is a little bit old-fashioned to EARN some of the nice things in life. Advertising agencies sponsor innumerable contests in which large sums of money, new cars, television sets, and vacation trips are offered--all for a boxtop, a soap wrapper, or a four-line jingle. The once popular TV quiz program worked itself out of existence with its unbelievably huge stakes and resulting dishonesty. Sometimes, women almost feel cheated to have to buy a box of detergent at its regular price, especially if there was a special bargain sale on the product last week! If you look around you'll see a dozen ways in which we are all affected by the same desire--to get a little more for a little less work, less time, less money, less effort. Is it any wonder that young people are growing up thinking that the world owes them everything.

There is a divine law in the Bible which cannot be ignored. "Whatsoever a man soweth, that shall he also reap" (Gal. 6:7) or, to put it in common language, "Whatever a man works for, that will he get." Second Corinthians 9:6 says, "He which soweth sparingly shall reap

also sparingly; and he which soweth bountifully shall reap also bountifully." I wonder if maybe a lot of us are trying to enjoy the distinction of being happy, useful Christians without paying the price? True, salvation is free but a life filled with the power of the Holy Spirit comes with a cost--poverty perhaps, or misunderstanding, or separation from loved ones, and a life of prayer. David said, "Neither will I offer burnt-offerings unto the Lord my God of that which doth cost me nothing" (II Sam. 24:24). What about you? Are you trying to get something for nothing?

Company's Coming

Do you like to have company? I do--now--but I remember with horror the first important company I had at my house right after I was married!

We had invited Don's aunt and uncle from the farm to have dinner with us and I had carefully planned days ahead of time what I would serve and how I would serve it. I was so anxious that everything be just right; you know how a bride wants to make a good impression on the in-laws!

My first problem came with the dessert. I had planned to have angel food cake with strawberries and whipped cream. When the cake came out of the oven it was about two inches high and as tough as it could be. The rest of the meal was not much better. The mashed potatoes were sticky and the gravy was lumpy. The jello didn't come out of the mold right. I can't remember what happened to the vegetables, but I'm sure they weren't particularly a howling success either!

The final defeat came with the meat. I had bought an expensive beef roast and felt at least somewhat satisfied with the way it was cooked. Too late I found out that Uncle Mel could not eat roast beef! Besides that, our tiny apartment was extremely hot from the cooking and the makeshift table we had set up in our living room made our meal crowded and uncomfortable. I think I finally dissolved into tears before the whole affair was over. Fortunately, Don's family was wonderfully understanding and they acted as though they had eaten the most expensive meal served at the Waldorf-Astoria. I've had some failures since, but none seemed as heartbreaking as that one!

Since I have been married I've developed a new appreciation for my mother and her hospitality. Guests have always been as welcome in her house as her own children, and there is no way of estimating how many hundreds of friends, strangers, and folks in need have eaten at her table. Many came who had been invited days ahead of time, but just as many, and perhaps more, were warmly welcomed who arrived unexpectedly when there was not time for much preparation. I used to get all upset if the house

39

was not nice when unexpected company arrived, or if the meal prepared were not a fancy one. If Mom was nervous, she never showed it. She picked up the house as best she could and calmly served whatever she had fixed--whether it was sirloin steak or sauerkraut and wieners. Sometimes she had to fry a few hamburger patties or open a can of beans at the last minute to make the food go around, but there was nearly always plenty.

Some of the guests were distinguished ones --college presidents, famous preachers and great singers, but there were many others who were not. I remember especially a Catholic girl who wanted to know how to get her prayers answered, an old man who thought nobody loved him, a missionary candidate who got appendicitis and had to stay for days, and a young Negro student from British Guiana who came quite regularly and affectionately addressed my mom as "Mother."

Hospitality is a wonderful privilege. In the first place, it enriches one's own life and broadens one's own horizon. It will teach your children to be gracious and hospitable. Their exposure to preachers and missionaries, espe-

cially, may be the influence that in later years will send them into the ministry or mission field. In the second place, hospitality is required of those who would be effective, blessed Christians. Hebrews 13:2 says, "Be not forgetful to entertain strangers: for thereby some have entertained angels unawares." In Romans 12 the consecrated Christian is commanded to be "given to hospitality" and in Titus a bishop (in our day we would probably say "pastor") is required to be a "lover of hospitality." You'll notice the Bible doesn't restrict the privilege and responsibility of entertaining to those who have special gifts along that line. Nor does it limit the command to those who have lovely homes or money for expensive food.

Don't worry about that worn place on the rug, neighbor. Just put on the coffee pot. Company is coming!

Camping

Have you ever lived with 100, 150 or 200 children all at one time? We had that unique and wonderful experience last summer working at a Christian camp just across the Wisconsin border. Don directed the two weeks of younger boys camp, taught Bible classes during the girls camps and helped occasionally with the music while I was in charge of the handcraft shop. Our little Carol and Jimmy got their fill of sunshine, water, fresh air and chipmunk-chasing!

Psychology books always list the traits characteristic of children of certain ages but I've never seen a description of that metamorphosis through which boys and girls go in one week of camping.

The boys always arrive at camp with shiny faces, brand new crew cuts, wearing their best pair of jeans. The little girls usually come with their hair in curls or in smooth, waving pony-tails and in starched blouses and well-shined shoes. The picture changes drastic-

ally before the week is over. The little boys hair is full of sand, their pants are soiled and torn, their sneakers smelly and their skin covered with sunburn, scratches and mosquito bites (some even add a little poison ivy for variety). The story is just about the same for the girls except that their hair, after a week of sun and swimming, begins to take on a mop-like appearance. I'm sure that more than one mother has been shocked and horrified to find that most of the clothes which she prepared and packed so lovingly at the beginning of the week come back without having ever been mov-

41

ed from the suitcase. One father was especially upset when he discovered that the plastic
bag which he had prepared for his son contain-
ing soap, washcloth, toothbrush and toothpaste
hadn't even been opened the whole week!

And then the dining hall reveals another interesting view of children away from the watch-
ful eye of the conscientious parent. A little
girl who is a "problem eater" at home gobbles
camp food like a hungry bear under the influence of lots of company, laughter and the activity and fresh air of camp. The boy who (with
his mother's encouragement) would never eat a
meal without washing his hands, sees nothing
unsanitary about bringing his can full of tree
toads to the table at camp. All the rules about
not reaching across the table, not talking with
one's mouth full, and not eating with one's fin-
gers--are broken in the camp dining hall in
spite of the best efforts of the counsellors and
directors.

On the other hand, there are some tender
and precious moments any parent would be
thrilled to witness--some unprecedented display of kindness and loyalty to a homesick bud-
dy, an unusual demonstration of good sports-

manship, the look of pride on a boy's face when
he says, "I got a letter from my dad!" or the
tearful smile of a little girl when she says,
"My mother will be so glad to know I've given
my heart to Jesus."

Whether we always like to admit it or not,
our children represent us, perhaps more truly
when they are away from us than when we are
close enough to control their words and actions.
Fortunately, camp counsellors, school teachers and others who work very closely with
children usually assume that the standards of
the parents are at least a little higher than the
children always manage to meet!

Before you get too nervous about your children and how they behave away from home, here
is another point to ponder. The Bible says that
we are "strangers and pilgrims" (or "campers"
if you please) away from our Heavenly Home
and Father. We are the representatives of our
spiritual family. Unfortunately, the world is
not so tolerant in assuming that our heavenly
calling is any better than our earthly walk. If
we claim to have a righteous Father, they have
a right to expect a certain amount of righteousness in us.

Blue Monday

This isn't Monday; it's Tuesday. But if ever I woke up with a "blue Monday" feeling, it was today. In the first place, I have a cold--the kind that makes my eyes red and swollen, my head throb, my nose runny and my body achy. In the second place, I was up half the night with my children--all three of whom also have colds, so no doubt I seem as impossible to them today as they do to me! Then to make matters worse, my dirty windows are staring me in the face, practically begging to be washed, and a great big mountain of ironing looks at me accusingly from the kitchen table.

If you are like me, your first impulse in such a situation is to crawl back into bed and pull the covers up high--leaving the children to their own devices! However, since my oldest is three and a half and my youngest five weeks old, that is a luxury in which I dare not indulge. I have to keep the vaporizer going for baby Donny, tie endless shoelaces and wash dirty

Once in a while I hear someone complain, "Well, they expect me to be so different, just because I am a Christian." What about it? Haven't people a right to expect more of us if we claim to know the Lord? As I've heard my dad say so many times, "A Christian ought to act different, look different, and even smell different from other people." Paul said, "Be ye therefore followers of God, AS DEAR CHILDREN" (Eph. 5:1).

How about you, fellow camper? Have you taken your spiritual soap and washcloth out of the suitcase recently?

faces, make sure Jimmy and Carol have on their sweaters when they go outside, referee their disagreements, patrol their endless trips to the kitchen or bathroom, and try to keep some kind of order in the house at the same time.

Just about the time I start feeling sorry for myself (me with my comfortable home, my kind, patient husband, and so many conveniences to make the work easier), I remember some of the letters from my reader-friends. Many of these are women with problems too numerous to name and to them my "blue Tuesday" would no doubt seem like a summer holiday! But regardless of how desperate and discouraging any day may seem, a Christian can find a cure for the blues.

When I was a freshman in college I returned from a 21-day college choir trip to California completely exhausted and at my wit's end. I had gotten too little sleep and drunk too much coffee (since that was just about the only beverage served) and I returned home to a pile of makeup schoolwork which seemed insurmountable. One night while I was practicing for my piano lesson it all seemed like more than I

could handle. I slammed both hands down on the piano and burst into tears. My wise daddy made me skip school the next day even though I protested tearfully that I couldn't possibly afford to miss another day of school. I was just too far behind in my schoolwork. In the morning Dad took me golfing. I had never played the game before but the fresh air and the walking did wonders for me. In the afternoon we hit a tennis ball back and forth in the street. That night I ate a huge supper, took a hot bath and went right to bed. I hadn't opened a book the whole day but somehow it didn't seem important when I went to bed--I slept like a baby. I think that one day, completely apart from my regular routine and problems, kept me from a nervous breakdown.

Now, of course, with the responsibilities of a family, I can't usually take off for a day. Still, I find that the same techniques do help to keep me from going to pieces when the going gets rough. Most things take on a different perspective after a nap, a change of jobs, a pleasant phone conversation or even a hot cup of tea.

Music does a great deal to help me through

a blue day. Many wonderful and comforting things have been written in prose and poetry, but when the heart is despondent and discouraged, the words which are set to music seem to slip into one's heart most easily to give comfort and calm. Sometimes I have been too discouraged to really pray and too tired to get much out of reading God's Word. That is when the words of some blessed song have their greatest value. I remember a time when the words of the song, "Peace, Perfect Peace" meant so much to me--especially the verse which says:

Peace, perfect peace. By thronging duties
    pressed—
To do the will of Jesus: this is rest.

Perhaps the best cure for "moody days" is to have made some preparation ahead of time. To have a great deal of Scripture tucked away in one's heart and mind is like having one's spiritual medicine cabinet well stocked for any emergency. If I am pressed above measure with work, I will probably not take the time to search for a verse or portion of Scripture which will give me rest; if I am too discouraged or tired, I probably will not make the effort to look for some verse of comfort and encouragement. The answer, then, is to have some passages from the Bible already memorized and ready for recall.

Well, I must stop this chatting and get back to my work. Maybe that ironing isn't so big, after all!

45

"That Look on Your Face"

The other day I was doing a job I never have cared much for. I was going through the toy-box, trying to decide what toys should be thrown away, given away, repaired or merely put away for awhile. We don't buy many toys for our children but with a large collection of kind and loving relatives, plus a couple of especially sweet and doting baby-sitters, our children have collected enough toys to supply several households! I felt a little guilty at having acquired so much, frustrated in my attempts to decide which toys should go where and a little provoked with the children who protested that each toy I was about to discard was their favorite. Besides that, it was already noon and I knew I ought to get lunch ready before the baby woke up and insisted on being fed.

Right in the middle of my confusion and hurry I suddenly realized that little Carol was looking at me very intently. "Mommy," she said quietly, "You've got that look on your face again." I suppose if she had said it in any

other way I would have wanted to spank her for impudence, but her worried expression proved that she didn't mean it that way. When it was called to my attention I could almost feel the hard lines of the scowl on my face. I hastily explained to her that I wasn't really angry--just tired and in a hurry--and then decided that I had better do something about "that look" on my face.

Have you ever sat on a streetcar or in a train station and watched the expressions on people's faces? Most people wear that pre-occupied look of care so common to all of us. Their eyes are dull and empty and their mouths droop. An expression showing anticipation, joy, or just plain contentment is so rare as to make other people stare. Our most normal reaction to the sad countenance of the world is to comment, "Well, what do you expect? They don't know the Lord." But if you've ever sat in a choir and watched the congregation of a good, sound, fundamental church you've probably been horrified or amused at the blank, dull look on so many faces. (Maybe I ought to add that quite a few choir members show the same expression!

46

My husband, who directs the music at our church, says that it is almost ridiculous to watch people singing, "Sunlight, sunlight in my soul today . . ." and all the time their faces are saying, "Stormclouds, stormclouds in my soul today . . .!" It is almost as though our singing were a ritual or form which we go through because it is required--not because we enjoy it or really mean it.

I never see people singing with deadpan expressions without getting a little heart-hungry for the Sunday School class of little Negro boys and girls I used to teach during college days. When they sang the chorus, "I'll Be a Sunbeam for Him," the room glowed almost literally-- their faces lit up so!

You know, it's a funny thing about children-- how keenly they observe the grown people they see day by day? If you've ever worked with young people you'll know that they comment on everything you wear, everything you say or do. One woman I know, who was superintendent of a beginners department for years, always wore only the brightest, frilliest dresses to Sunday School because it mattered so much to the children who saw her.

But how much more closely do they watch our faces! When the little girl prayed, "Lord, make the bad people good, and the good people nice," I rather think she was referring to the sour look so many of us "good people" wear. Children are literal and candid in their observations. If the Bible says, "The fruit of the spirit is love, joy, peace . . ." then they expect us to look loving, joyful, and peaceful. Perhaps they occasionally think we are liars. Can it be that we are? In Isaiah 29:13 God says, "This people draw near me with their mouth, and with their lips do honour me, but have removed their heart far from me." Perhaps that's what is wrong with our faces--something is wrong inside.

And what about the reaction of people who don't know the Lord? I'm sure that more than one unsaved person has been repelled because of the somber, disinterested expression on the face of some Christian. Are you guilty?

Come on now, friend. Someone is watching you--smile!

A Family Christmas

I'll tell you very frankly, I am almost child-ish about Christmas. Every year I can hardly wait to see the tarnished old decorations being hung from the lightposts of our little suburban town and to listen for the lovely carols which pour out of the loudspeaker right in the middle of Main Street. I still get goosebumps when we read Luke's account of the nativity around the lighted Christmas tree, and misty-eyed when I hear little children sing, "Away in a Manger" at the church Christmas program.

I love the laughter that rings through the house while we plan our Christmas surprises and wrap our gifts and the squeals of delight when each surprise is discovered and each gift is opened. I love the way everybody acts at Christmastime--store clerks seem more pleasant, neighbors more sociable, children more courteous and the world just a little less skeptical and disillusioned. I love the fellow-ship and the feasting--the smell of the rich brown turkey in the oven, the pumpkin pie and the cornbread; the special joy of being together with those I love best.

Our family Christmas traditions follow pret-ty much the same pattern year after year but it still all seems exciting and wonderful to me. Christmas Eve we spend with the Sandbergs in Moline and then early Christmas morning we drive back to Wheaton to spend that day with my side of the family. In Moline we will have a smorgasbord with many of the traditional Swedish dishes and lots of good midwestern American food as well. After that there will be Christmas carols and the reading of the biblical Christmas story and then the opening of all the dozens of gifts. Afterwards there will be coffee and cookies before we all go to the 11:00 p.m. service at the church.

On Christmas day our celebration with the Rices will be just about the same as it is every year except that there will be a few more ba-bies (three new ones this year!), a little more noise, a little more food, and the old home-stead will seem just a little bit smaller than last year. We will have our annual family "program" in which everyone has to take part --a song perhaps, or poem or Christmas reading, and we will probably all recite Luke's Christmas story together. Then we will each take turns telling what we are most thankful for this year. Afterwards there will be gifts and laughter, a thankful kiss here and there as each package is unwrapped. Someone will probably run upstairs to try on a new dress and no doubt we will all have to stop occasionally to look for a doll shoe or toy car which has gotten lost in the mountains of Christmas wrappings. After all the mess is cleared away and the new treasures packed away in the cars, we will all play games and talk and eat some more!

Of course, with such a large family there is always someone with some special burden or need, and occasionally a family Christmas has been shadowed by some particular sorrow or grief. Sometimes a few of the loved ones are far away or someone is ill. Still, the blessed part of the whole celebration is that no matter where we are or whatever the burdens, the precious Lord Jesus, whose birthday we celebrate is ALWAYS with us and so we can say, and really mean, "Joy to the world, the Lord is come!"

CHRISTMAS AT "THE RICES"

Tall, expectant, stands the old house,
   Clean and garnished, waiting for
Happy greetings, warm embraces,
   Children's footsteps at the door.

Fragrant smells from kitchen oven
   Promise fare too good for kings--
Fat brown turkey, cornbread dressing
   Baking while the kettle sings.

Every family arriving
   Adds a treasure to the fare:
Fruitcake, hot bread, sweet potatoes--
   How the good smells fill the air!

In the living room o'erflowing,
   Packages and boxes pile.
Little fingers, poking, feeling,
   Are absorbed in childish wile.

Soon the table, all extended,
   Will be weighted down with food.
Thanks are offered, plates are loaded;
   Hearts are in a joyous mood.

49

Now the festive meal is ended,
Dishes washed and put away.
Happy conversation blends with
Children's laughter, bright and gay.

Dad, in custom oft repeated
Reads again the story old.
Luke's familiar, precious message
Thrills again as when first told.

Carols, testimonies telling
Of God's grace throughout the year,
Stories, poems, perhaps a reading,
Prayers of thanks that all are here.

Now it's time to open presents.
Squeals and shouts of glad surprise,
All rewards for time and effort
Can be found in others' eyes.

Hearts are full, the day is ended,
Loving wishes then expressed,
Each one goes away repeating
That "This Christmas was the best!"

--Jessie Rice Sandberg

A Salute to Old Age

The other day we had some friends at our house whom we hadn't seen for about ten years. You know what the reaction is when you see people you haven't been with for so long a time. After that first thrilling greeting, you ask each other questions about what each is doing, admire the ever-present pictures of the children, comment on the news about other mutual friends and then you begin to reminisce about old times. At that point it is somehow easier to think of oneself as that earlier, more youthful person--the one you used to be ten years ago without the added weight, the deeper lines around the eyes and the graying hair.

We live in such a paradoxical world. Young people try harder and harder to look like, act like, and be treated like older people. If you have a thirteen-year-old daughter, you have probably heard her say that "everybody" (notice, please, that I use quotation marks) her age has a pair of high-heeled shoes; a seven-year-old boy will tell you that "most" of his friends own cars; and it is a matter of public record that an increasing number of young men are already raising families by the time they get their college degrees. More and more, it seems, young people are trying to take on the sophisticated ways of the adult world.

On the other hand, older people are working just as hard to simulate the attributes of youth. Magazines, radio and television proclaim loudly or subtly an innumerable number of aids to make us all feel and appear more youthful-- everything from skin creams and hair tints to reducing pills and "figure controllers." It is considered a special compliment if people say, "You haven't changed a bit!" or "Oh, but you COULDN'T be a grandmother!"

We might as well admit it: most of us really do not enjoy the prospect of being old. Actually, I doubt if it is the physical frailty of age that we dread as much as it is the stigma that society in our day has placed on old age. We have developed such a veneration of youth and physical beauty that old age has become something almost to be ashamed of. We forget to appreciate the value of acquiring a whole lifetime of experience, of knowledge; the understanding one learns of people; the satisfaction of being able to put material things in their proper perspective (an attribute that seems to develop almost exclusively with age); the patience learned in having experienced sorrow and pain and disappointment--all of these blessings which are the walking companions of maturity.

In a famous modern novel about China, an ancient oriental grandfather describes our western world as a strange place "where turnips grow upside down; where women learn to read, and where youth is venerated instead of old age." In many places of the world the oldest member of the family is still treated with respect and honor as head of the clan. How strange it would seem to them to see so many of our old people tucked away in county farms for the aged--some without even the rarest letter or visit from the children to whom they have given life.

I have in front of me an article (clipped from a recent issue of Everywoman's Family Circle Magazine) called "Let's Stop This Silly Worship of Youth." In it there is a quotation by Dr. Dan W. Dodson, director of New York

University's Center for Human Relations and Community Studies, in which he says, "In my work at the center I have noted a definite over-emphasis on youth and glamour, and this is not only an unrealistic but an unhealthy attitude. It tends to make young girls so self-centered about their appearance that they have difficulty adjusting to their roles as normal human beings. And it makes women not of the youth group feel inferior."

And then if there were no other reason to be grateful for old age, it would be sufficient reason just to have proved that God loves and

'The Bible, which is by all odds the final authority, has something to say about youth and age too. Leviticus 19:32 says, "Thou shalt rise up before the hoary head, and honour the face of the old man, and fear thy God: I am the Lord." There is a warning in I Timothy 3:1 that a bishop should be "not a novice, lest being lifted up with pride he fall into the condemnation of the devil." And in Titus 2:3, 4 the aged women are instructed to be "teachers of good things; That they may teach the young women to be sober, to love their husbands, to love their children . . .'"

cares for His own. My Grandmother Cook died six years ago at the ripe old age of 87. In the last few years of her life she often gave a testimony which included the following words from Psalm 37: "I have been young, and now am old; yet have I not seen the righteous forsaken, nor his seed begging bread."

Well, who's afraid of a little gray hair?

52

It's Morning

Morning is a wonderful time of day. I don't mean that first horrible fifteen minutes after the alarm has gone off when you're still struggling between sleepiness and wakefulness. The part I like begins when the teakettle begins to whistle and the table is already set for breakfast. By then I usually feel awake, hungry and sociable.

One of the nicest things about morning is that it follows pretty much the same pattern day by day. I like that secure feeling of knowing just what I ought to do next--fix breakfast, have family devotions, prepare Don's lunchbox, wash breakfast dishes, make the beds and dress the children. From then on the activities and duties vary from day to day. Then comes that struggle in my mind about whether it is more important to scrub the kitchen floor, do some sewing or catch up on correspondence.

Another nice thing about the first part of the day is that we are all still fairly nice to live with! The problems and cares of the day have not yet begun to make us discouraged and cranky. Even our pre-schoolers who wake up with a bounce, just bubbling with good will, usually get a little tired and fussy later in the day; so I especially enjoy those happy hours of the early morning.

The third thing I enjoy about mornings is the quiet fifteen minutes or so we spend having our Bible reading and prayer together. No matter how hectic or busy the rest of the day is going to be, that part at least I can count on to be calm and refreshing. I don't mean to give the impression that our family devotions are never threatened by outside distraction or unexpected interruptions. If it isn't Captain Kangaroo beckoning invitingly from the TV set, it is a telephone call or that ever-present dictator of our lives--time--that attempts to rob us of the most precious part of our family life. Probably the biggest enemy of family worship is a change of routine. For example, we find our Bible reading is likely to suffer on Saturdays when we eat later or when there is company in the house for breakfast or on those rare occasions when for one reason or another we don't sit down to the table together.

53

I think if I were asked to give suggestions for making family devotions really work I would say that the two keys are (to borrow a phrase from a well-known women's magazine) "togetherness" and "time." We might as well face it--families who do not eat their meals together will in all likelihood find it impossible to have regular family devotions. Mealtime is the hub of the family; it is the most compelling reason for drawing a family together at one time. For that reason it is probably the best time for family worship. Bedtime would seem to be a logical time but actually children are often too tired to be responsive then. Besides, there is always the possibility that one or more members of the family will have to be away at that prescribed hour.

The other key to making family devotions work is to allow enough time in the daily schedule, even if it means the whole family has to get up fifteen minutes earlier. Once everybody gets the idea that Bible reading is as unchangeable a part of the day as dressing is, then it really isn't too hard to stick to the routine. The system fails when you let every late night

out or even occasional early appointments rob you of this time together.

At our house the children are present for family devotions even though they are too young to read or to understand all that is being read. They often follow the portion of Scripture we are reading in THE BIBLE IN PICTURES FOR LITTLE EYES by Kenneth N. Taylor (Published by Moody Press, Chicago) and we explain as much of the Bible as we are able. But whether or not they grasp all that we read, they still sense the importance of the reading, because we MAKE it important. The amazing thing is that they do catch more of the meaning than we would think possible.

Do you like mornings? Maybe there is something missing. Have a REALLY good morning. Read the Bible!

Beginning Again

Aren't you glad for new beginnings? I don't suppose there is a night when I don't go to bed wishing I had done something differently or wishing I could live over some minute or take back something I have said too hastily. My children sometimes say, after a particularly mischievous or fretful day, "Mommy, I'm sorry I was bad today. Tomorrow I'll try real hard to be good."

What if there were never any forgiveness for the failures of this minute, this hour, this day; no forgetting the disappointments and frustrations of yesterday or last week or last year? How wonderful that God gives us lots of opportunities for fresh, new beginnings. There is always a new morning, a new week, a new year. One can always hope, and better yet, pray that "tomorrow will be different." Just think how discouraging it would be if life were a timeless sort of existence without any starting places for beginning again.

We all need to run our lives like a good housekeeper does. She tries to keep up with the dishes and dusting and washing and ironing every week, but once or twice a year she goes over the whole house from top to bottom and sees that EVERYTHING is fresh and clean. The curtains have to be washed and starched, walls and woodwork washed, shelves cleaned, rugs shampooed, windows washed and furniture polished. Our hearts need the same kind of attention. There is always some daily cleansing required, but once in a while it is good to ask the Lord to go over us real good to see if there is some sin lurking in a far corner that we've been missing in our "heart housekeeping."

In spite of all the jokes made about New Year's resolutions I always make them--every single year. Naturally some of them are broken eventually--some very soon, but would anyone dare to say he was better off for having never made any holy resolves, any prayerful attempts to do better? Little children do not learn to read or tie their shoes or dress themselves without practice and "starting over." And so is it true that regular habits of Bible study and prayer often have to be "set" again after periods of carelessness and backsliding. I frequently have to ask the Lord to give me grace to guard my tongue. And repeatedly I need to "begin again" to be the careful, patient mother I ought to be and want to be. It isn't quite enough to have made that decision once. With every failure (and how many there are!) there has to be, in a sense, a starting over.

And then there are always resolves I need to make about trying to win certain, definite people to the Lord--the milkman perhaps or the paper boy, a lost neighbor, or maybe even a member of my own family. So often we hope, or pray in a detached sort of way that these will be saved, but in most cases we won't do anything positive about leading them to the Lord unless we first make prayerful resolves to work at winning them.

The Bible is full of instances where men of God have made resolutions. Joshua said to the people of Israel, "And if it seem evil unto you to serve the Lord, choose you THIS DAY whom ye will serve . . . but as for me and my house, we will serve the Lord" (Joshua 24:15). David said, "So will I sing praise unto thy name for ever, that I may DAILY perform my vows."

All of us need to make some new covenants with the Lord or renew some old ones. We dedicated our Carol and Jimmy to the Lord when they were tiny babies, and now our little Donnie will be dedicated next Sunday. Don and I will pledge to raise our baby for the Lord and win him to Christ early in life. But we find that over and over again we need to remind ourselves and the Lord that our children still belong to Him. When Hannah presented her little boy Samuel to the Lord she vowed, "For this child I prayed; and the Lord hath given me my petition which I asked of him: Therefore also I have lent him to the Lord; as long as he liveth he shall be lent to the Lord." Hannah eventually had three sons and two daughters, but since I am a mother too, I feel sure that occasionally in the night she wondered, "Is my little Samuel well? Does he miss me?" I think it is not unscriptural to assume that many times in those years while Samuel was growing up and when Hannah's heart was hungry for that special child, she had to renew the vow she made when first he was given to the Lord.

I don't know what resolves you need to make. Perhaps many of them are, like mine, too personal to mention to anyone but the Lord. Let's pray, shall we, that we'll have the courage to make some resolutions and that we will have the Lord's help in carrying them out.

"It is of the Lord's mercies that we are not consumed, because his compassions fail not. They are new every morning: great is thy faithfulness" (Lam. 3:22, 23).

"Mommy, I Don't Like My Sins!"

A very solemn and frightening yet wonderful thing happened at our house this week. I'm not sure what your reaction will be as I tell you, but since it so closely concerns me and mine, I find it difficult to even talk about it without a lump in my throat.

Our little Carol Joy, who will be four on the seventh of February, woke up in the middle of the night crying because she had had a bad dream. I comforted her and prayed with her and soon she was fast asleep. The next afternoon I was busy getting the children cleaned up and planning an early dinner because it was Wednesday, which is our regular night for church prayer meeting. Carol wanted me to do something for her but, because I was in such a hurry, I told her she would have to wait. Suddenly she said, "Well, I don't like you anymore. I'm going to get me another Mommy!" Almost before I had time to be horrified at that unheard-of outburst she broke into tears, threw her arms around my neck and said, "Oh

Mommy, I'm sorry! I don't like to say things like that!"

Later that night as I was tucking her into bed, she asked if I would pray with her again that she wouldn't have any more bad dreams.

"Well of course I will, honey," I said, "but what was it you dreamed that frightened you so last night?"

"I dreamed Jesus wasn't going to take care of me anymore!" and with that she burst into tears again. In between sobs she added, "I don't like my sins. I don't want them anymore. I want to be in Heaven with Jesus, too!"

Now if you are like me, you probably decided long ago that a child does not reach the age of accountability until he is at least five or six. And so you can imagine how shocked I was to realize that a little child, not quite four, could feel such terrible conviction of sin. True, she had been in Sunday School and church regularly, had seen us read the Bible together and pray for lost sinners, but somehow I was still taken off guard at her urgent need for forgiveness of sin. Yet, who would dare to say this was NOT the conviction of the Holy Spirit?

I explained to my little girl as simply as I

58

could that Jesus died to take away our sins and that all she needed to do was to ask Him to come in and make her heart clean and white. Then we both prayed and her prayer sounded for all the world like some hard old drunkard coming to the Lord after a lifetime of sin! (I don't mean to make light of this, but I rather think the Lord smiled a little tenderly when He heard her, just as I did.) She seemed relieved to have it all settled and soon was fast asleep.

The story doesn't end there. And this is the part that makes it especially sweet and thrilling. The next morning Carol came running happily into the kitchen and said, "Mommy, I didn't have any bad dreams. God did hear us pray, didn't He?"

I have hesitated to tell you this because, as I said, I have had some preconceived ideas about how much of spiritual truth a young child is able to grasp. For several years I taught a Sunday School class of beginners and I finally gave it up because I had that frustrated feeling that they were too young to understand very much of the Bible. Now I wonder, did those eager, earnest little boys and girls understand more than I gave them credit for?

I think I am aware now, more than ever before, of the tremendous privileges and responsibilities of training little children. What I say to you I say to myself, mother or Sunday School teacher: Don't be discouraged and above all, don't be careless with the souls of the little children left to your keeping. Some tender young heart may be waiting even now for Jesus to come in and you may be the only one who will have the chance to open the door!

All About Hands

What kind of hands do you have?

When Don and I were in our courting days we went to a party where a most unique game was played. All the girls were placed behind a huge drape where holes had been cut for the hands to go through. Each fellow had to iden- tify the hands (minus any rings, watches or other telltale paraphernalia) of the girl he had brought to the party. Of course the behind- curtain giggles probably helped in the identi- fication but it was still surprising how quickly each girl was recognized by her hands.

Surely there are as many varieties of hands in the world as there are faces. Tall, slender people usually have long slender fingers. A stocky, athletic man is likely to have broad, square hands. There are people with extra long thumbs and extra short little fingers--such an infinite variety in hands!

Sometimes you can tell a little about what a person does by looking at his hands. One of the loveliest girls I know is a gifted pianist and her hands have a muscular look resulting from

years of hard practice on the piano. Women who have spent a lifetime doing careful and delicate needlework sometimes have knuckles that are gnarled almost to deformity. Printers and auto mechanics may bear nearly permanent marks of their trade under their fingernails and in every pore of their hands.

Often the spirit of a person can be seen in his hands. I have a warm, animated friend who can hardly carry on a conversation without using her hands. She not only tells the story with her lips; she illustrates it with the move- ments of her hands! And have you ever noticed that a firm handshake usually goes with a con- fident personality and a hesitant one with a timid personality? My husband says that when he was a little boy his grandmother would sometimes help him wash his hands and be- cause her hands were so gentle they seemed to him to be the softest, loveliest hands in the world. The hands of idleness--whether long and slender or square and fat--wear a badge peculiar to themselves, no telltale redness from the dishpan or broken nails from scrub- bing pots and pans or knobby knuckles from heavy work either indoors or out.

One of my favorite stories concerns the 14th century German artist, Albrecht Durer, who became known around the world for his engravings and drawings. The story goes (and I am sorry I do not know its source) that Durer had a less gifted brother who worked many long and difficult hours earning a living for both of them while Albrecht studied to become an artist and engraver. After many years, when Albrecht had won his fame he did the etching of "Praying Hands" using his brother's workworn hands for his model. It seems some kind of poetic justice that thousands of people who would not even recognize the name of Albrecht Durer are familiar with and love the beautiful "Praying Hands."

I have just finished reading again the 31st chapter of Proverbs where the virtuous woman is described so beautifully. Several times her hands are mentioned in the passage. First, that she "worketh willingly with her hands." Second, that she "layeth her hands to the spindle, and her hands hold the distaff." Third, "she stretcheth out her hand to the poor; yea, she reacheth forth her hands to the needy." And then this wonderful chapter closes with these words: "Give her of the fruit of HER HANDS: and let her own works praise her in the gates."

Well, then, never mind if your hands are a little chapped and red from too much hot water and soapsuds, or stained with peeling potatoes, or calloused with your mending. Perhaps they are, after all, the most beautiful hands of all!

A HOME PRAYER

"Lord of all pots and pans and things,
   Since I've no time to be
A saint by doing lovely deeds
   Or watching late with Thee;
Or dreaming in the dawnlight
   Or storming Heaven's gates,
Make me a saint by getting meals
   And washing up the plates!

"Although I must have Martha's hands
   I have a Mary mind,
And when I black the boots and shoes,
   Thy sandals, Lord, I find!
I think of how they trod the earth,
   What time I scrub the floor;
Accept this meditation, Lord!
   I haven't time for more.

"Warm all the kitchen with Thy love,
    And light it with Thy peace!
Forgive me all my worrying
    And make all grumbling cease!
Thou who didst love to give men food
    In a room or by the sea,
Accept this service that I do--
    I do it unto Thee!"
                --Author Unknown

An Open Letter to Anne

Dearest Anne:

I just received the newspaper clipping which said that your little Jeanne Anne, so joyfully expected, died at birth. My heart has been especially heavy since I remembered that the doctor had said this must be your last baby.

The temptation is for me to say, "I know how you feel because of the baby we lost . . ." but in reality that is slim comfort. No one can completely fathom the depth of another's sorrow and loss because there is no yardstick to measure grief. Still, there is that precious promise from the God of all comfort, "Who comforteth us in all our tribulation, THAT WE MAY BE ABLE TO COMFORT them which are in any trouble, by the comfort wherewith we ourselves are comforted of God" (II Cor. 1:4). So, whether or not my experience is exactly the same as yours, we still have the same Lord, and so I can promise you, there IS comfort for sorrow.

I suppose one of the greatest blessings of

losing a loved one is that Heaven is never again quite so far away nor is earth ever again quite so sweet. The more treasure we have on the other side, the more eagerly we can look for the dear Saviour's coming. Our houses and possessions, our daily preoccupation with "getting ahead," our frustrations and worries all seem to become less important than they did before. And you have already found, I know, that the Word of God is more precious than you have ever known it could possibly be. I remember how sweet the Bible was to me as I read it through that first long night after our baby died. Now, in any time of doubting or distress I have only to go through those same tear-stained pages to be reminded again that God is still the "Father of mercies...the God of all comfort."

Isn't it a blessed thing to realize that the Lord KNEW He could trust you with trouble? Not everyone has a chance to "taste and see how gracious the Lord is," nor could the Lord count on just anyone to bring glory to His own name in any time of testing. I know you can take this as a precious privilege given in mercy, and you will be amazed at the opportunities the Lord will give to use this experience to be a great blessing to others.

Several years ago, a friend of ours (a consecrated and busy young assistant pastor) was killed in a tragic highway accident when his baby boy was only three weeks old. Afterwards, when I went to visit his wife, she told me with a glowing face how wonderfully the Lord had used her husband's death in telling others about the goodness of the Lord. There was no questioning, "Is God fair?"--only that calm assurance that His way was best. I left with the feeling that I was the one being comforted and reassured. Since then I have found that the promise, "As thy day, so shall thy strength be," really is true for the Christian. The doubting and disillusionments about the goodness of God usually come from people on the outside looking in--not from the one who suffers the loss. There is a certain sacred fellowship with the dear Saviour which is to be found only in sorrow--a thing which the world cannot possibly comprehend.

I wish we were there with you and Lee right now, but I know you have many who love you and will be helping you. Do take the time to rest until you get your physical strength back. This will be a good time for your beautiful Becky and sweet Sharon to take over and learn to be "mamma."

Don sends his love too. He is, in fact, sitting at the piano right now playing "God's Wondrous Grace." Remember how many times we sang it together and always got goosebumps when we came to that beautiful part:

". . . For Jesus came to set my
    troubled spirit free--
Eternally I'll sing God's wondrous
    grace!"

May this be true of you today. I'm enclosing a poem by Paul Pastnor which really sums up all I've been trying to say. I pray it may be the blessing to you it has been to me:

LEAN HARD

*"Cast thy burden upon the Lord, and
he shall sustain thee"--Ps. 55:22*

"Child of My love, lean hard,

And let Me feel the pressure of thy
    care;
I know thy burden, child, I shaped
    it;
Poised it in Mine own hand; made
    no proportion
In its weight to thine unaided
    strength,
For even as I laid it on, I said,
'I shall be near, and while
    she leans on Me,
This burden shall be Mine, not
    hers;

"So shall I keep My child within
    the circling arms
Of My own love.' Here lay it
    down, no fear
To impose it on a shoulder which
    upholds
The government of worlds. Yet
    closer come;
Thou art not near enough. I would
    embrace thy care;
So I might feel My child reposing on
    My breast,

Thou lovest Me? I knew it. Doubt
not then:
But loving Me, lean hard."

Much love,
Jessie

Something in Common

My sisters and I have sometimes been ac-
cused (and rightly so, I'm afraid) of having so
much fun together that we were hardly aware
there was anyone else in the room! When six
girls grow up together, play together and fight
together, share each other's clothes and secrets and even occasionally each other's boy
friends, there is bound to be a certain close-
ness even after each is happily married and
busy with a family and life of her own.

The truth of the matter is that we do have a
great deal in common even with our differences
in personality, work and interests. We were
raised strictly but lovingly, and so our convictions are basically the same. We all went
to the same college and had many of the same
teachers, knew the same people. When any of
our husbands achieve any special honor or success, we are all as pleased as if the success
were our own. If Grace composes a piece of
music, or Mary makes a lovely dress, or Libby
has a book published, or Joanna prepares a

65

Front row, left to right: Mrs. Grace MacMullen, Mrs. Lloys Rice, Dr. Rice, Mrs. Elizabeth Handford.

Back row, left to right: Mrs. Joy Martin, Mrs. Joanna Rice, Mrs. Jessie Sandberg, Mrs. Mary Lloys Himes.

66

beautiful meal, or Joy has a solo part in a cantata, we shamelessly brag about each other to anyone who will listen. We usually laugh at the same jokes, read the same books and enjoy the same kind of music. Sometimes we share financial burdens, or baby-sitting services, or even occasionally, advise. We feel free to discuss our opinions and theories on absolutely everything under the sun in the presence of each other. It all boils down to the fact that we have something in common: we are sisters, we were raised together, we understand each other and love each other.

Isn't it a wonderful thing to find someone with whom you have something in common? I have sat in the waiting room of a doctor's office with a dozen other women (each with her own brood of squirming, crying babies) where all of us arrived as complete strangers. But, because we all had babies, it wasn't long before we were all comparing feeding problems, telling how early our own children walked or talked, and so on--discussing a dozen other subjects of common interest to mothers with young children.

Sometimes we have something in common with people because we work at finding a common interest. When I was in high school I liked a boy who was a Brooklyn Dodger fan. Almost without realizing it I (who had never been to a professional baseball game in my life!) had learned the names of nearly every important player on the Brooklyn team. Because I liked the boy I managed to get interested in the same things he was interested in!

Some of us don't have very much in common with the Lord Jesus so we really are not very comfortable in His presence. We go to church only when it is convenient and we do not find any special joy in fellowship with others who love Him. We read His Word so seldom and so carelessly that it becomes a bore--like reading a letter from a stranger--without any sweetness or blessing for our own hearts. Because He is no special, personal friend of ours, we don't particularly care whether anyone else gets to know Him and love Him either. Prayer is a ritual which we go through because it is expected and becomes a sincere petition only in the direst need. By that time the relationship is so strained we feel no assurance that He has heard or wants to answer our prayers.

How sad this is when you consider how much the Lord did to have something in common with us. He became a tiny baby, born of human flesh, learning to walk and talk and work with His hands. He grew up feeling hunger, weariness, pain, loneliness, poverty and ridicule-- all so that He could share our feelings and needs. If ever a person sought to find a common interest with those He loved, it was Jesus!

Is your friendship with the Lord Jesus a little cold today? Maybe you need to renew some common interests and get re-acquainted with that Friend of friends. Discover again this blessed fact:

"For we have not an high priest which cannot be touched with the feeling of our infirmities; but was in all points tempted like as we are, yet without sin. Let us therefore come boldly unto the throne of grace that we may obtain mercy, and find grace to help in time of need."
--Heb. 4:15, 16.

A Word in Season

Once in a while I get the urge to "put on the dog" for my husband when he comes home from work. I'm sure you know the routine. I fix the food he likes best and then add a couple of extra trimmings to make the meal really special. The tablecloth has to be a better-than-everyday one and the centerpiece something more than the artificial flower arrangement that usually sits on my table. I get the house looking spic and span, put the evening paper by his armchair and turn the lights just so--to make everything look inviting and comfortable. After that I put on a fresh dress and fix up a little bit myself and then last of all (for obvious reasons) I clean up the children. The results are usually so satisfying, the evening meal so festive, I end up wondering why I don't go to that extra bit of effort every day.

But then occasionally something goes wrong like it did a couple of weeks ago. The house was in order and the dinner was done. The children, scrubbed and shining, were waiting expectantly at the front window for the sight of Daddy's car coming up the drive. Five o'clock came and went, with no sign of Daddy. By 5:15 the children had given up the vigil and were already pulling out the toys we had put away for the day. At 5:30 I turned off the oven on the roast which was looking a little dry and put the lids back on the already cooling vegetables. The Jello salad which as yet hadn't begun to suffer from the delay was put back into the refrigerator. At six o'clock I was beginning to be a little worried and annoyed that my usually punctual husband could be so late. At 6:15 the children were becoming dishevelled, grumpy and hungry. My dinner looked like last week's leftovers.

I was just conjuring up a mental picture of the wounded expression I would wear . . when the door opened, and there stood my husband. Before I had a chance to act offended that my lovely surprise had been ruined, he grinned mischievously and said, "How come dinner isn't on the table." His boyish and yet shrewd good humor so threw me off guard that I got tickled and that spoiled any intentions I may have had to appear upset! (In fairness to my husband and to all really thoughtful husbands, I must explain that his delay was, after all, a completely unavoidable one!) I warmed the less-than-perfect dinner and we all sat down to eat with relish.

There is a special blessing in learning to say the right thing at the right time. Misunderstandings are healed, arguments are ended, peace is restored, when words are spoken thoughtfully. Proverbs 15:1 says, "A soft answer turneth away wrath: but grievous words stir up anger," and then further on in the same chapter, verse 23b adds, " . . . a word spoken in due season, how good is it!"

My husband has another choice comment he uses on me when the occasion demands it. After I've been up half the night with sick or wakeful children, he sometimes greets me at breakfast with a cheerful, "My, but you're looking beautiful from such a good night of sleep!" Of course we both know I look bleary-eyed and exhausted but that little bit of foolishness helps to get my day started right.

I know a young lady who has a way of stopping gossip dead in its tracks just by the way she answers when anybody is discussed critically in her presence. If someone complains about what a terrible housekeeper Mrs. So-and-so is, she adds quickly, "Oh, but have you ever noticed how much she does for her neighbors?" If the pastor is taken to task because he neglected his weekly visit to some ailing church member, she will say, "But did you realize how many unsaved people he visited last week?"

Some people say, "Well, I could never be a soul winner because I don't have the gift of gab," when actually the thing which brings a person to the Lord is usually not a quantity of well-chosen phrases. People who seek to win the lost by a great display of biblical knowledge probably will do nothing more than impress a lost sinner with his learning. How much better to offer "a word fitly spoken"--a simple and urgent invitation to accept Christ given with the Holy Spirit's power.

And then there are times when no word at all is better than any number of choice explanations. When we were growing up and had disobeyed our folks or had gotten into trouble of some kind or another, my dad used to say, "No alibis will excuse doing wrong." For some

reason we always thought "explaining why" would make it all right. That temptation isn't limited to children. If you've ever done personal work in jails or prisons you know that practically every man there will say, "It wasn't really my fault. . . ." Isn't it strange that we all want to justify our actions as though a multitude of words could make our black hearts pure!

Occasionally I find myself yelling at my children or trying to argue them into behaving when perhaps a brief-but-in-earnest spanking would be twice as effective and half as painful for all of us! There is a real value in learning what it means to speak a word "in due season." Let's give our manner of speech a good going-over, shall we?

"Let your speech be alway with grace, seasoned with salt, that ye may know how ye ought to answer every man." --Col. 4:6.

Touchy Christians

Any time I see some old friend from my high school days at Wheaton Academy, one subject always comes up which has brought me endless embarrassment and chagrin. It was years before I could recall the particular incident mentioned and laugh--really, sincerely laugh.

My senior year I was a member of the Academy Gospel Team which traveled around to churches in the local area presenting a program of gospel music and a brief message. At the time I always sang a very low alto either in a trio or duet--never as a soloist. One particular Sunday night our team was invited to a church in Chicago where we presented our usual program and then turned the service over to the pastor for the closing invitation.

The preliminary part of the meeting had gone along without a hitch and I was just breathing a little sigh of relief as the pastor asked the congregation to turn to the invitational hymn, "Just As You Are, Come Home," in the hymn-book. Even though I had practically learned to walk in the sawdust aisles of revival tent meetings, that was one song I had never heard of! Instead of trying to sing the first verse along with the congregation, I listened rather distractedly and wondered if anyone would be saved.

The first verse of the song came to a close and somewhere in the fog of my inattention I heard the pastor saying quietly, "Miss Rice, will you please sing the second verse?" I gulped in horror. Not only was the melody part far too high for my inexperienced voice, but the song was completely unfamiliar and I hadn't listened to a word of the first verse. I was so scared the music became one big blur! Frantically I clutched the arm of the girl who sang soprano in our trio, and begged in a hoarse whisper, "Here, you sing it, please. He MUST mean you!" She kept her eyes closed and stubbornly shook her head "no." By that time the pianist had already sounded an insistent opening chord and I struck out in the weakest, most wobbly voice you ever heard. I doubt if I hit ten notes right in the whole stanza. The only thing that I was aware of was that the horrible squeaking I heard was my own voice and that my classmates to the right and left of me were so convulsed with laughter they made the bench shake.

A woman was saved that night, believe it or not, right in the middle of that pitiful second verse, but I was so buried in my own humiliation and wounded pride, I didn't even care. I was furious with the quite innocent pastor for asking me to sing, indignant with my friends for their perfectly natural teenage giggles, and sick with embarrassment at the mess I had made. I privately vowed I'd never do another thing in public as long as I lived. I certainly didn't intend to put myself in a position again where people could laugh at ME!

Fortunately someone eventually reminded me that the only thing seriously injured was my own pride and that the world would probably go on just about the same whether I sang well or not! It all boiled down to the fact that I hadn't honestly been singing to serve the Lord in the first place. I was merely enjoying the chance to exploit my own self-importance. Still, as I said, it took several years for me to learn to laugh whenever the story was told.

I'll have to confess that my ego still gets tender-skinned pretty often. Oh, not in such obvious ways, of course. I've had too much practice trying to APPEAR humble and spiritual. But what is it, if not pride, that makes flattery so sweet to my ears, or candid, honest criticism so hard to take? Why is it so many of us have to be flattered and cajoled into doing what we ought to do humbly, yet willingly for the Lord? Any pastor or Christian worker can tell a dozen instances where he has had to baby along "mature" Christians in doing real sincere work for God. How often have you heard someone say, "Well, be careful how you approach such-and-such. You know how easily offended she is," or worse yet, "So-and-so would be a good Sunday School superintendent except that he is so touchy he's a little hard to work with"?

Now that I've dragged out my dirty linen, let's get personal about you. When you are asked to sing in the choir or teach a Sunday School class or tell a flannel-graph story, do you simper sweetly, "Oh, no! Really, I couldn't. I'm not talented," and all the time you are hoping someone will just beg you to do it? Do you sometimes think people don't appreciate your value to the church? Do your feelings get hurt pretty often? Don't tell me; just test your own heart. Maybe you need to post Psalm 119:165 over your kitchen sink or at your desk, or especially in your heart:

"Great peace have they which love thy law: and nothing shall offend them."

Is There a Baby in the House?

I've just been sitting here and thinking (with a little bit of a sigh) how obvious it is to anyone who enters any room of my house--that a baby lives here.

First, of course, a visitor would see the scratched and chewed playpen blocking the doorway between dining-area and kitchen, then his eye would quickly take in the highchair with a soiled bib still hanging from one side. With only a little more investigation he would discover the cribs and teddy bears and diaper pail and vaporizer and boxes of tissues. Depending on the time of day there might be the betraying odor of baby powder or wet diapers or warming cereal. And of course there are the dirty marks made on walls and woodwork by tiny fingers, the nicks in our once-proud furniture and the litter of baby things throughout the house-- all clear evidence of the little ones who live here.

Perhaps the least expected yet most earth- shaking change in a home with the coming of

73

babies is that one's whole manner of living is different. Mealtime, once enjoyed leisurely and without interruption, suddenly becomes a beehive of commotion--children's chatter and spilled milk, grape jam on the tablecloth, scoldings and coaxings until the last green bean is chewed and swallowed, and then finally when everyone else is finished, a plate of cold food to be eaten alone. Every hour of every day is punctuated with childish arguments that have to be settled, paper dolls that have to be found and toy trucks that have to be fixed, and every single day holds its share of kisses, smiles, spankings, band-aids and scoldings-- all of which must be bestowed in unbelievable quantities.

Even nighttime holds no sacred barricade against the intrusions of children. A drink of water, a pat of comfort after a nightmare, blankets to be tucked in again and again, sometimes a whole night spent rocking a feverish and fretful child--all of these are part of the price of bearing children.

Having described the clutter and disorder and informality that necessarily go with having babies in the house, the next obvious question

would seem to be, "Well, are they worth it?"

Don't ask the woman whose life is absorbed in parties or travel or clothes or lovely possessions or in any other involvement, no matter how worthy--who has not had children. As the saying goes, "Ask the lady who owns one!" If you have ever pressed a fuzzy baby head against your heart, or watched the first brave attempt of a baby hand struggling with a spoon, or heard a rosebud mouth lisping "I love you," then there is only one answer: "Yes, yes, a thousand times, yes!" Babies are worth every forsaken ambition, every sleepless night, every sacrifice of beautiful things, every moment of precious time.

Now let me ask you another question. Have you ever been in a church where there were no baby Christians? I have been. The stained-glass windows and the glistening oak pews were wonderful to behold. The robed and well-trained choir sang beautifully. The pastors' sermons (sound in doctrine and in perfect English) were eloquently delivered. The congregation was made up of only the "best" Christians, many of whom served admirably on any number of church boards and committees. The air of respectability which surrounded the church and its people was rarely contaminated by even the slightest breath of scandal. Everyone said that church was a real credit to the community. But something was missing. There were no baby Christians. No tears of repentance, no bad habits to be broken, no dirty lives to be changed and made over, no halting testimonies of God's wondrous grace. How sad to be in a church whose walls, however beautiful, are never hallowed by the birth cries of a sinner being born again.

True, spiritual babies, like natural ones, sometimes cause inconvenience and sacrifice. Profound and eloquent preaching must sometimes be sacrificed for the simple, urgent gospel messages that cut the heart. Even the music must be geared to the needs of the simple and ignorant as well as to the needs of those who have loved and served the Lord for many years. Sometimes even our most cherished formalities and trappings must be put away so that any lost soul, no matter how impoverished or uneducated, will feel welcome. Babies always have to be fed milk, handled carefully and given a great deal of love. Some-

times they stumble and fall. Often they require special encouragement as they learn to walk, learn to feed themselves from the Word of God, and learn to take the responsibilities of being a member of the family of God. But just ask anyone who has ever been in a church where people were constantly being saved: "Is it worth it?" To feel the warm breath of revival spread throughout the congregation, to see a hardened sinner pleading for mercy at the altar, to see whole families changed and blessed, to hear lips once full of profanity sing the praises of the Lord. Yes, yes, of course it is worth it!

Tell me: Is there a baby in the house?

Jimmy's Pawpaw

At Christmastime Pawpaw and Grandmother Rice gave our two-and-a-half-year-old Jimmy a toy shaver. It has a tiny battery inside and when it is working right it makes an authentic-sounding buzz just like Daddy's shaver. The only trouble is that some little wire in it is not now fastened quite right, so there is no buzz. When I told Jimmy I would see about getting it fixed, he said, "No, Pawpaw will fix it." I reminded him that Pawpaw had to be in India "where the tigers are" for a long while and that he would have to be gone down South for a while longer and that it might be quite sometime before Pawpaw could get around to fixing the shaver, but still he insisted, "No, Pawpaw will fix it."

It doesn't matter to Jimmy (or to his other fifteen cousins, for that matter) that Pawpaw is a very busy man. They are aware that he preaches to get people saved and that he writes books and songs and has a radio program, but as far as they are concerned he is their dear

Pawpaw and that is the most important thing about him! They know they can visit him at his office anytime of the day to get a hug and kiss, and maybe even a cooky. When they eat at his table they fight to sit next to Pawpaw and they think nothing of asking him to cut their meat or spoon up their soup. They crawl in and out of his lap as they please, play with his hair and take his time to share any number of childish confidences.

Some of us who are a little older and "wiser" know what a tremendous load of responsibility he carries and so we often feel a little uneasy about taking up his time with the sort of trivia which our children share with their granddad. And yet, sometimes I wonder if life wouldn't be a little lonely if none ever needed us in the small things of everyday life. Certainly, the tying of a shoelace for a little child bespeaks a more loving, personal relationship than would the giving of a large sum of money to some remote, unfamiliar charity, no matter how worthy. Without a doubt, the most precious of all human relationships are those in which there is sympathetic and loving interchange of ideas and desires and needs, no matter how important or how trivial. We all need someone who is deeply interested in our affairs and who solicits that same interest from us.

Then think how God must feel.

He who holds all the secrets of life and death and time and space and eternity craves to hear the childish prattle of our petty little prayers. You say, perhaps, "Well, I don't want to bother the Lord with anything that isn't really important." Now let me ask you: What can you share with the Lord that really IS important? Can you give Him advice as to the spacing of the planets or the speed at which they should rotate around the sun? Can you add anything to His wisdom concerning sin, righteousness or judgment, or will your opinions in any way alter the character of His holiness and mercy? Of course not. But the blessed fact of the matter is that THAT is not the kind of fellowship God expects or wants of us.

Jimmy's Pawpaw will not consult with Jimmy in the management of all the various ministries of the Sword of the Lord Foundation. But that doesn't mean Pawpaw and Jimmy have no common ground for warm mutual fellowship. Whatever is lacking in Jimmy's knowledge or vocab-

ulary or interests, Pawpaw more than makes up for. All Jimmy needs to bring to this sweet relationship is his need and love for his grandfather. That is all any good granddad would expect, and with that the friendship is complete.

Jesus said in the most profound and yet simplest of words, "Whosoever therefore shall humble himself as this little child, the same is greatest in the kingdom of heaven" (Matt 18:4). Maybe you've been insulting God's intelligence by presuming that He needs you for your wisdom or your goodness or your "Christian maturity," when what He really desires is a childlike dependence and love. What a shame to miss the blessing of sharing your every confidence, of carrying to Him your smallest, most insignificant needs and feeling the sunshine of His smile reserved especially for His own dear child!

Summer Is Coming!

It is 3:45 p.m.

It has been a lovely winter's day. From my kitchen window I can see the school children on their way home, some skipping, some dawdling over a puddle, others trudging along together, laughing over some private joke of their own. The sun is still smiling proudly at his handiwork of the day--snowbanks melted down to almost nothing and tiny rivulets of water running beside our street. Even though the shadows are becoming horizontal and the distant hills are taking on the lavender cast of evening, the air still wears that spring-like feeling we've had all day. The sub-zero weather of a week or two ago already seems like ages past. We are almost deceived into believing that winter is nearly over.

I have just been thinking how much of our lives are judged by comparisons. For example, this day which I have enjoyed so much is lovely because it comes as a sharp contrast to this season when the days are usually dark, the

wind has a cruel bite to it, and all the wonders of our Illinois vegetation are locked beneath a blanket of ice and snow. But should we have such a day as this breaking into the perfection of a lovely summer the story would be different. Our 40-degree temperature would not seem warm after all. The gray-green of the grass peeking now through the last vestiges of yesterday's snow would seem ugly by the lush green hues of June. The black naked trees (a comfortable and familiar sight in the winter-time) would look ghastly and out of place in a summer landscape. Even this sky, with its bright winter sun, would probably look a little forbidding in the setting of a warmer season.

Spiritually, too, this old world is wrapped in the cold darkness of winter. So many of our dreams are like the bare trees--empty and fruitless. We seem to be constantly beaten down by the bitter winds of criticism and disappointment. All the good things we hope to do with our lives often seem to be frustrated and frozen by our own weakness and sin and buried under the banks of discouragement and disillusionment. Even though we know the Sun of Righteousness is in the sky, His face is often hid by winter clouds of despair and so we cannot feel the warmth of His presence.

And then suddenly, in the middle of our heart's cold winter, we feel the soft, summer breath of revival. The sun smiles down in warming rays and here and there the hardness of men's hearts begins to melt. Our prayers, so long unanswered, break through the hard ground like spring blossoms and our ambitions and endeavors, cultivated and planted so long ago, begin to bear fruit in that brief taste of summer.

Sometimes, after a period of refreshing and blessed revival, we are disappointed to discover that what we have enjoyed is not really summertime yet, only the promise of what Glory will be like. We still have to face more icy blasts, more frozen dreams, more dark days when we cannot see God's face.

True, winter is not quite over but how good the Lord is to give us, now and then, that sweet taste of what eternity will be like in the endless presence of the Lord Jesus. And how doubly wonderful to realize that the very best of God's blessing here will seem like darkest winter compared to the flawless perfect fulfillment of fellowship with Him in the summertime of Heaven.

Does the winter seem long and cold, Christian? Take heart; summer is coming!

I Was a Stranger

Once in a while, when I get to telling myself how much entertaining I would do if my house were larger or my furniture newer, I remember something which happened in my college days. The choir of which I was a member was on tour in the East and we had just finished a concert in a tiny little church high up in the mountains of Pennsylvania. There was no hotel nearby and the members of the church had very kindly made arrangements for the various choir members to stay in the homes of the church people before leaving the next morning for our next concert.

My roommate and I were assigned to the home of a coal miner seven miles away from the church. On the way there our host told us, in broken English, that he had worked on hands and knees in the mines since he was a young boy, newly arrived from Italy. He also said, modestly and yet without embarrassment, that although his home was not a fancy one, our visit had been anticipated with a great deal of

80

joy and that he was sure his family could make us comfortable and happy. (I suppose he sensed the misgivings we felt. To tell the truth, I HAD pictured a mining village with dirty shacks and rough, uncultured people.)

Up to a point, the little mining settlement was just about as I had pictured it. The frame houses provided by the mining company were exactly alike. I have tried unsuccessfully to remember if there were electric lights. My impression is that there were not. I know there were no indoor bath facilities, no telephones, no central heating. When I stepped from the car my comfortable world of familiar, taken-for-granted luxuries seemed mighty far away!

But then something happened. The door opened into one of the warmest, most pleasant kitchens I had ever seen. A large, glistening coal stove stood prominently at one end of the room. The linoleum on the floor absolutely sparkled with cleanliness and the neat curtains were starched and clean. A sweet-faced lady introduced herself as our hostess and then she gently pulled a little boy in front of her who had been shyly hiding behind her skirt. "This is our son," she said. "He has looked forward so long to having you here that he is almost sick with excitement. I couldn't get him to eat a bite all day."

From that moment on I wasn't even aware of time or surroundings. That lovely Christian family treated us as though they thought we might be angels unawares. They somehow anticipated every possible need or desire we might have had. Before we went to bed that night we were served fresh hot coffee, warm homemade bread with jam and butter. It was a perfect bedtime snack, just exactly what we wanted, but I think that if we had asked for broiled lobster they would have tried to get it for us. By the time we left the next morning we felt they were dear old-time friends. Their warm hospitality given in the name of the Lord Jesus had bridged all the differences in background, in age, in interests or way of life. We were strangers but we had been treated as honored, especially beloved friends.

In the years since, I have been in many lovely homes and have enjoyed the hospitality and kindness of many, many friends. Yet somehow I am still haunted by the remembrance of the coal miner and his family who made us feel so welcome, though we were complete strangers. I wish I had known some obvious, tangible way to say "thank you." I have thought much about the message Elisha sent to the Shunammite woman after she opened her home so graciously to him: "Behold, thou hast been careful for us with all this care; what is to be done for thee?" (II Kings 4:13).

The blessed thing about doing any service for the Lord is that He provides the reward whether it comes through human sources or not.

"Then shall the King say unto them on his right hand, Come, ye blessed of my Father, inherit the kingdom prepared for you from the foundation of the world: For I was an hungered, and ye gave me meat: I was thirsty, and ye gave me drink: I was a stranger, and ye took me in: Naked, and ye clothed me: I was sick, and ye visited me: I was in prison, and ye came unto me. Then shall the righteous answer him, saying, Lord, when saw we thee an hungered, and fed thee? or thirsty, and gave thee drink? When saw we thee a stranger, and took thee in? or naked, and clothed thee? Or when saw we thee sick, or in prison, and came unto

81

thee? And the King shall answer and say unto them, Verily I say unto you, Inasmuch as ye have done it unto one of the least of these my brethren, ye have done it unto me." --Matt. 25:34-40.

Go Quickly and Tell!

Have you ever heard the saying, "If you want to advertise, tell a woman"?

Just between us women, I've always been a little curious as to why our sex as a whole gets so much pleasure out of sharing news and confidences. Now maybe you are not made as I am, but I'll confess I just love to be able to call up a friend and say, "Guess what! Mrs. So-and-so had a seven pound baby girl this morning." There is something fun about hearing the voice on the other end of the line say, "Oh, really! How wonderful! How did you hear?"

I know, of course, that this natural characteristic of women sometimes degenerates to something less than noble. All too often we are guilty of dusting a little soot on somebody else's reputation by what we say, whether by dropped hint, a vague inference, or, God forgive us, sometimes by a direct, malicious intent to hurt. Any time a conversation includes the phrase, "Don't pass this on, but . . ." you can be sure something has been said which shouldn't have been! Evidently this temptation so common to women appeared long before the telephone or the backyard fence. Paul warned Timothy that young widows, supported by the church and not having enough to keep themselves busy, might become "tattlers also and busybodies, speaking things which they ought not."

Fortunately, any God-given attribute (as we will assume a woman's gregarious nature to be) has its good points too. After the angel announced to Mary that she was to be the mother of Jesus and that Elizabeth was also expecting a child, Mary could hardly wait to visit Elizabeth and to share their common joy. I've often wished I could have eavesdropped on those two women as they no doubt discussed at length the miracle which had happened to Mary and the remarkable blessing to Elizabeth. How exciting it must have been for them to share those secrets which the world had no capacity for understanding.

One of the sweetest parts of the resurrection story is, to me, the fact that the women who loved Jesus were the first to find out that He was alive. For once, no one said, "Now keep this to yourself. . . ." Instead the angel said, "Go quickly, and tell his disciples that he is risen from the dead." Then just a little bit later when the women saw Jesus in person He repeated the word, "Go tell my brethren . . . ." Somehow it seems more usual that the task of telling would have been given to Peter or James or John. No wonder the story which the women told with such fear and joy seemed to the disciples as "idle tales." Who would have expected THAT exciting message to be delivered first to women! Surely a woman's desire to be "first with the news" was never more wonderfully or completely satisfied than on that day!

Have you been telling the good news? It is just as much our privilege and responsibility to tell today as it was to those women so long ago. Can it be that the wonder and thrill of the fact that Christ is alive has gotten to be old stuff? Have we forgotten that every promise in the Bible is guaranteed by the fulfillment of Jesus' resurrection? Are there no "Hallelujahs!" in our hearts this Eastertime?

Well, then, don't just sit there, neighbor--

go quickly and tell! Here is news you can share
with the whole world!

"Go tell the story marvelous,
They need not die in sin;
Go tell the story marvelous,
Out Lord invites them in.
While untold millions wait untold
That Jesus saves from sin;
Let's go tell the story marvelous,
And bring them in."

Parking Meter Miracles

One of the great blessings of growing up in a preacher's family is that there are so many opportunities for contact with greatly used men of God. Some are known for their powerful preaching, some for their heart-stirring song. Some men are known for their ability to move Heaven and earth by prayer. "Pappy" Reveal, founder of Evansville Rescue Mission, was just such a man.

I will never forget how startled I was the first time I heard Dr. Reveal pray. His prayer had no formal beginning or end. At one moment he might be talking to those around him, then the next moment he was including the Lord in the conversation! In the course of his ministry he asked for--and received--many thousands of dollars for the work of the mission, the radio and the camp. At the same time, he consulted the Lord about the simplest matters, as a personal friend would consult a personal friend.

One winter time, I remember, as we were

getting ready to go from home to the mission for a service, he tapped his knee (he was a cripple for many years) and said, "Now, Lord, you know how tricky this bum leg of mine is and you know how icy the streets are; you just put your angels up there on the fenders to keep this car on the road!" Then he confidently started the car and we safely arrived at the mission.

Do you pray about everything? In our family a "parking meter miracle" is an answered prayer regarding some little seemingly insignificant matter of everyday life. It might be a lost umbrella which is found, a badly needed full night of sleep, a hoped-for letter from a distant loved one, or as our pet title above would indicate, merely a parking place on a busy downtown street. My brother-in-law, Walt Handford, says he not only prays for an empty parking place; he prays that there will be some time left on the meter as well!

Before you pass this kind of praying off as being foolish and irreverent, let me remind you of something. I have three little children, the oldest being four years old. So far, not one of them has ever asked for a winter coat to keep out the cold, a well-balanced meal, or a spe-

cial bank account to insure his or her college education. No doubt the day will come when these things will be important to them, and of course with God's help we hope to always be able to provide for our children. But because they are very young and very trusting, their requests seldom reach those proportions. Instead, they often ask for a cooky, a drink of water, a kiss, a little help in coloring a picture, a story to be read, a song to be sung. By asking us for the simple things, they learn to trust us and to ask us for the big things as well. What parent would brush a child away because his request is not important enough?

Psalm 103:13 says, "Like as a father pitieth his children, so the Lord pitieth them that fear him." The dictionary defines pity as "kindness, sympathy, compassion. . ." How blessed to realize that the Lord's heart is stirred with our deepest needs, but that also, because He is a Father, He knows and wants to fulfill our little day-by-day desires as well.

Just ask Him and see!

Green Roses

The next time I get to thinking I don't have to abide by some rule, I hope I have the good sense to remember my experience this week with the green roses.

It all started innocently enough with a shopping trip to nearby Oak Park. I was walking idly down the aisle of a department store when my eye caught sight of a demonstrator making big, gorgeous roses out of pink icing. I was fascinated. All my life I have had a secret ambition to be able to decorate cakes just like the professionals do--with roses so lifelike you can almost smell the perfume.

I watched wide-eyed and openmouthed as the lady, with a mere flick of the wrist, turned out dozens of confectionary masterpieces. It looked so easy I was already picturing myself as the cake-decorating marvel of the neighborhood. When the saleslady announced that the entire professional-type kit could be had for a mere one dollar, I wasted no time reaching into my purse for the cash.

I could hardly wait to get home and try out my new toy. There were no birthdays coming up, but I decided I could just go ahead and make my roses, put them in the freezer and wait for a chance to put them on a cake. The instructions were clear and simple . . . . "one tablespoon of butter to one cup of confectioners sugar . . . add a few drops of milk if needed." I started out as the recipe said with one tablespoon of butter, but as I added the sugar the batter began to look very dry.

"That recipe just can't be right," I said to myself. "Why, I can't even get the butter and sugar to stick together. I'll just add a little more butter and milk." Which is exactly what I did. When the frosting LOOKED the right consistency I added pink food coloring to part of it, and green coloring to the rest. But somehow, once the frosting was in the pastry tube it didn't seem half so thick. Instead of spinning out beautiful pink roses with realistic green leaves, the tube oozed out small blobs of pink and green goo which resembled nothing. Of course I had to scoop it out of the tube again and add more sugar . . . and more sugar . . . and more sugar still. By the time my frosting really WAS thick enough I had great piles of the pink stuff and three times that much of the green! I made green leaves, green rosettes, green birds nests and green roses by the dozen, before I used up all that awful green frosting! By the time I was through I had the whole kitchen filled with sheets of waxed paper covered with all sorts of little green concoctions. Needless to say, I learned (I hope permanently) that recipes usually mean what they say!

You probably are thinking, "How foolish of you not to follow the recipe right from the start." Of course I was foolish, and without excuse, too, since I'm not exactly a bride anymore. By now I should know the perverse qualities of confectioners sugar. But the point is, I THOUGHT I knew better.

Yes, it is foolish not to follow a recipe in cooking, but how much more foolish to ignore God's tested and tried recipes for blessed, Spirit-filled Christian living. The Word of God is full of formulas to make our lives happy and successful, and generations of God-fearing men and women have proved that they work. But how often have you or I read some command or promise in the Bible and thought, "Well, that sounds fine, but I don't think it applies to me." About tithing, for instance . . .or prayer . . . or obeying our husbands . . .or spanking children. We excuse ourselves by saying, "But I think MY case is a little different."

How silly to have a kitchenful of unneeded, unwanted green sugar roses. But how much sadder to have a life full of frustrated plans, unanswered prayers and powerlessness with family and friends--all because we refuse to follow the recipe.

"Be not deceived; God is not mocked: for whatsoever a man soweth, that shall he also reap."--Gal. 6:7.

Words Without Meaning

Isn't it wonderful how children love music? My children try to repeat almost every song they hear. Of course the words are often garbled or ignored completely but the melody and the time nearly always come through perfectly. When Carol (now four) was just a tiny little thing, she sang "Jesus Loves Me" in such a mixed-up fashion, I could never hear her without laughing. This was her version:

> "Jesus 'uve me, dis I know
> Fo' da Bible tuddie-toe,
> 'Ittle ones to Him be young,
> Dey are works but He is stwong."

And then just the other day I heard her singing: "Whosoever shirley mee-na-mee, shirley mee-na-mee, etc. (Translation: "Whosoever surely meaneth me.") When I asked her if she knew what the words meant, she just shrugged and smiled self-consciously. At Christmastime our two-and-a-half-year-old Jimmy sang his favorite, "Away in a Manager" very sweetly but I was always startled when he ended the chorus with "The little Lord Jesus, asleep on his head."

I remember one or two songs I learned as a child which had to be re-learned after I understood the meaning. The chorus, "Safe Am I" was one of my favorites and since I learned it by ear I thought one of the lines began "Shelter door . . ." rather than "Sheltered o'er" as the author intended.

It is perfectly natural for children to enjoy words without meaning. The varieties of sound are new and wonderful and the discovery of their own power to articulate is even more exciting. It would be asking almost too much to expect them to grasp the meaning of every word just as fast.

But for a grown-up, and especially for a Christian, words without meaning are almost inexcusable. Let me illustrate. When I was in college we used to have a chapel service every morning at 10:00. I made a practice of coming in, sitting down and bowing my head in silent prayer before the service began. One particular day I came in following my usual

88

pattern of bowing my head, only this time I caught myself silently mouthing the words, "Dear Lord, we thank you for this food . . ." I looked up shocked and embarrassed, almost wondering if I had been heard. The principle of regular prayer was right but I had so relegated the act to habit that my heart was really a million miles away. My disinterested subconscious mind had just taken over and put on the wrong record! I was saying words without meaning.

I'm glad we have no way of knowing how many lies are spoken in prayer meetings and song services. It just might put the church out of business. Perhaps the reason so many of our prayers go unanswered is because the Lord knows we really don't mean what we are saying. And I wonder if perhaps there are times when our lies, no matter how beautifully sung, so nauseate God that He wants to cover His ears. How often have you sung, "Only to be what He wants me to be, every moment of every day . . ." or a similar song when you honestly meant just that? Knowing my own heart, I dare say the experience has been rare.

Now I'm not suggesting that we cut out half the hymnbook, or the praying either, for that matter. But I do think it is time we search our hearts and resolve to do as I Corinthians 14:15 says: "I will pray with the spirit, and I will pray with the understanding also: I will sing with the spirit, and I will sing with the understanding also." Let us see that the Lord never has to say of us, "This people draweth nigh unto me with their mouth, and honoureth me with their lips; but their heart is far from me" (Matt. 15:8).

Loneliness

Have you ever had the experience of feeling terribly, completely alone?

A couple of summers ago the Rice clan planned a rare week of vacation together up in northern Wisconsin. At the time, all the families except ours were living in Wheaton, so we were especially excited at the prospect of being together with everyone. As it turned out, the only week in which the majority of folks could get away, was a week in which my husband was already committed to direct a boy's camp--we couldn't be with the others. Our disappointment was softened by the fact that Carol and Jimmy (both very small) and I would get to be with Daddy at the camp, so that we at least would have that much sunshine and fellowship with each other.

En route to Camp Willabay we stopped in Wheaton long enough to wave good-by as the carloads of happy vacationers pulled away from the curb. Later, when we arrived at the camp, both the children were a little fussy and

Jimmy had begun to feel feverish. By morning their hot little bodies were completely covered with red spots. Here we were at a camp with 150 little boys, sporting two full-blown cases of measles!

Don, of course, had to stay at the camp, but we knew we would have to take the babies somewhere so that the campers would not be exposed. I dreaded driving two very sick children the nearly 200 miles back to our home, so we finally decided I should take them to my folks' house in Wheaton, only 65 miles away. I tried to appear confident and cheerful as I kissed my husband good-by, but I really felt mighty blue. Jimmy had developed a severe earache besides being already uncomfortable and feverish, and so he wailed almost every mile of the way.

Somehow, when we got to Wheaton, the familiar town and the dear old house meant nothing with the folks who made them dear, so far away. The big silent rooms seemed almost strange as I went in and put my babies to bed with Jimmy's intense earache lasted throughout that first long night and he cried until he was exhausted. When he finally gave up and slept for a few fitful minutes, I laid down and cried my-

90

self, feeling that I was certainly the loneliest person in the whole wide world. Once my self-pity had spent itself, I began to remember the precious promises of the Lord: "Lo, I am with you alway . . . ." "I will never leave thee nor forsake thee."

As happens with most earthly problems, things got better. The children rapidly improved, the quiet lonely week wore away and soon we were happily re-united with all our loved ones.

It is a sad, frightening experience to be lonely. Somehow ambition drains away, initiative is sapped, and time becomes a weight almost too heavy to be borne. Sometimes loneliness has nothing to do with alone-ness. We can be lonely when we are surrounded by people. It is even possible to be lonely when we are surrounded by those who are dearest to us. To have your motives misjudged, your actions misinterpreted, your words misconstrued--to be misunderstood by someone you love is to experience the deepest kind of loneliness possible. And then there is a loneliness that goes with bucking the tide. Human nature makes us want the approval of the masses. It is not always easy to be a "nar-

row fundamentalist" when everyone else is being "broadminded."

If ever a man tasted loneliness to the deepest dregs, it was the Lord Jesus. Imagine dreaming of the heavenly Home, the light of the Father's smile, the loving adoration of holy angels, and then waking up to realize your bed is Judean sod, your companions ignorant and impulsive fishermen, and your destiny a cross of shame. That was real loneliness. And for what? So that our hearts need never again feel the loneliness and emptiness of sin. As the sweet little chorus by Audrey Meir says:

"... so I'll brush away the tears,
An forget my foolish fears;
I'll never be lonely again, never again."

The Good Old Days

I wonder what it is about human nature that makes us think the things we can't have are better than the things we CAN and DO have? Take the matter of time, for instance. The past always seems sweeter than the present. We remember with nostalgia "the good old days" and secretly wish for things to be as they once were. We long for the days when we could buy a good steak for 39¢ a pound, when there was no P.T.A. to require our attendance, no Community Chest to request our money or our time, and when a good book or a piece of needlework was a favorite means of entertainment. We bemoan the fact that today's young people are absorbed in cars and television and the latest hit records. We gripe about the luxury tax we have to pay on our jewelry and cosmetics, and we complain about the high cost of insurance we pay to protect our late model cars, complete with radio, heater and jet-spray windshield cleaner! We fuss at the high carrying charges we have to pay on our houseful of

luxuries, and when the repair man charges $4.00 an hour to fix the automatic washer, we throw a fit. All it takes to make us really mad is to have the boss require a couple of hours of overtime work, without pay!

In retrospect, the good old days seem mighty fine. We have long since forgotten the inconvenience of the coal oil lamp, the wood-burning cookstove, the outhouse, and the old metal washtub (in which we washed the clothes with homemade lye soap). We no longer remember the loneliness of being miles away from schools, stores, doctors, and the nearest neighbor; the backbreaking drudgery of doing all our housework with broom and scrub brush and an old-flatiron. We can hardly imagine that people once worked from sunup to sundown (without coffee breaks) six days a week and that there was no such thing as a two-week paid vacation.

What am I getting at? Just this: the ungrateful, foolish human heart seems to have no capacity for finding joy and contentment in things as they now are. Instead, we want to reach back to the past, completely ignoring all its disappointments and inconveniences.

In my daily Bible reading I've been taking special note of all the complaints of God's people. It is shocking to realize how many the Bible records. The children of Israel had barely gotten out of the terrible slavery of Egypt when they started murmuring, "Wherefore hast thou dealt thus with us, to carry us forth out of Egypt . . . ." Led by a pillar of fire, fed with manna from Heaven and sustained by miraculous water, clothed with garments that never wore out, and protected by the God of Heaven, they had the nerve to long for "the good old days." Even faithful Joshua, discouraged by the defeat at Ai, said, "Alas, O Lord God, wherefore hast thou at all brought this people over Jordan . . . ." How grieved the Lord must be with the discontent and ingratitude of His own children.

Paul said, ". . . I have learned in whatsoever state I am, therewith to be content. I know both how to be abased and I know how to abound: every where and in all things I am instructed both to be full and to be hungry, both to abound and to suffer need. I can do all things through Christ which strengtheneth me."

The most precious commodity you have are these very moments right now. The "good old days" are gone. You can't change them or bring them back. Let's thank God for the present, whatever its problems or privileges, and find contentment and joy in serving Him -- RIGHT NOW!

"Let your conversation be without covetousness; and be content with such things as ye have: for he hath said, I will never leave thee, nor forsake thee."--Heb. 13:5.

Insomnia

I am constantly amazed by the tremendous number of products on the market devised to cure the modern malady--insomnia. To invalids and other people who must be inactive much of the time, sleeplessness is a real problem. Pain can keep one wakeful for many hours. Worry is probably the greatest cause of insomnia. For some people, a late cup of coffee, an exciting evening, a stimulating discussion or an argument can keep them from settling down to sleep immediately. I dare say most people at some time or other in their lives have had some difficulty getting to sleep.

I think that King David must have suffered from insomnia. Perhaps the great sin into which he fell started with a restless night in which he walked the housetop trying to bring on sleep. Other Scriptures seem to indicate that David, weighted with the responsibilities of war and government, spent many wakeful nights. When David's heart was right with the Lord he

enjoyed the sweetest fellowship with God during those nighttime hours. In Psalm 42:8 he says, ". . . in the night his songs shall be with me, and my prayer unto the God of my life." In another place David says: "I have remembered thy name, O Lord, in the night . . ." (Ps. 119: 55). In the 63rd chapter of the Psalms, David tells the Lord, ". . . my mouth shall praise thee with joyful lips: When I remember thee upon my bed and meditate on thee in the night watches" (vss. 5b, 6). And finally he says, "Mine eyes prevent (meaning "anticipate" or "look forward to") the night watches, that I might meditate in thy word" (Ps. 119:148).

Often David used the night hours for times of confession and heart-searching. In the fourth Psalm he advised, "Stand in awe, and sin not: commune with your own heart upon your bed; and be still." In a time of great trouble, David said in heart-broken pleading with the Lord, "I am weary with my groaning: all the night make I my bed to swim; I water my couch with my tears" (Ps. 6:6).

Generally, sleeplessness is a wearying, discouraging thing, but it can be turned into something good and profitable. Our whirling, hurrying, busy way of life does not allow much time for Bible study and prayer, for meditation, for searching one's own heart, for quiet, private thanksgiving and especially not for dreaming one's own dreams. What a wonderfully sweet blessing it is when we can occasionally borrow an hour or so from the night hours to satisfy some of our heart's deepest needs. Then we do not wake up with the feeling of frustration over hours lost in wasted, wearying sleeplessness.

I always got a sort of secret pleasure out of having to be up for a 2:00 a.m. feeding when my babies were very small. It was nice to have a time that was completely my own without distraction or intrusion of telephone, visitors or home duties. Sometimes I memorized Scripture during those precious quiet moments, sometimes I prayed, and sometimes I just enjoyed the infinite sweetness of the nursing baby in my arms.

Some insomnia, I'll admit, is not pleasant, and some perhaps is not easily fixed. But if our wakefulness is produced by worry and doubt, then there is a cure--better than pills, or hot baths, or warm milk, or what have you:

"Offer the sacrifices of righteousness, and put your trust in the Lord. There be many that say, Who will shew us any good? Lord, lift thou up the light of thy countenance upon us. Thou hast put gladness in my heart, more than in the time that their corn and their wine increased. I will both lay me down in peace, and sleep: for thou, Lord, only makest me dwell in safety."--Ps. 4:5-8.

As the Twig Is Bent

Anytime I am around some particular age group of young people for a prolonged period of time, I find myself thinking, "Isn't that the nicest age to be?" Babies are so sweet and dependent, six-year-olds are so full of fun and wonder, pre-teens so unpredictable and exciting, and young adults are so courageous and so confident that they can solve all the world's problems, singlehandedly if necessary. (I must be moving out of this age bracket--I've already discovered there are several things I can't handle--either alone or plurally!) Each age is winsome in its own way. How thrilling it is to watch the variety of changes from birth to maturity!

In our summer camp work Don and I have had a chance to get to know many teenagers and post-teenagers and so that age group is beginning to find a certain special place in my heart. I love the blend of the childishness not quite gone and maturity not quite reached which is

the typical characteristic of the teen-age years. There is a certain beauty in a rose, no longer a tight little bud without individuality or fragrance, still not quite full-blown either. Such is the beauty of a teenager.

Several years ago a high school boy came to camp who was so unusually popular and still so unusually mature that he took the place by storm. Dave had all the most longed-for assets of youth--good looks, tremendous athletic ability, a pleasant personality and a complete lack of self-consciousness. He obeyed the camp rules and encouraged others to do the same. His enthusiastic spirit was so contagious as to be felt throughout the whole camp. Added to that, he was an earnest soul winner and won more of his fellow campers to the Lord than did any single counsellor on the grounds! No one was surprised when he won the award for Best All-Around Camper.

The next year his sister, Diane, came to camp and it was soon obvious that she had many of her brother's attributes. She was pretty and friendly and she possessed the same spiritual depth we had noticed in Dave. Later she came back to work on the staff as a waitress in the dining hall during the summer months. Though she was popular and fun-loving, she did the work well which was required of her and graciously accepted additional responsibility when she saw the need. Both brother and sister were ideal campers, outstanding young people, and we often conjectured that they certainly must have come from a fine Christian home. You can imagine my surprise when someone told me that Diane and Dave were trying to win their own parents to the Lord. "Win their parents?" I asked incredulously, "I thought that surely those two young people had come from an ideal Christian home. I've never seen young people who have been given better character training than they."

Gradually in the years of working with young people I have begun to discover that children of unsaved parents who have been given careful moral instruction and character re-inforcement have a better chance of turning out right than do children of Christian parents who have never been taught that sin does not pay, that disobedience must be punished. Sadly enough, godly parents do not always produce godly children. Stranger yet, sometimes unsaved parents, because they are conscientious about moral training, make it easy for other people to win their children to the Lord.

Spiritual training and character training ought to be synonymous terms. The biblical meaning of the word "spiritual" does include those attributes which denote "character." It is only in modern times that we have defined a spiritual home as being one where prayer is offered at the table, where church attendance is somewhat regular, where the parents enjoy a rather pleasant pious relationship with other Christians and a non-controversial one with the world in general. Unfortunately, this "spiritual" kind of home offers no guarantee that the children raised therein will grow up to love and serve the Lord. Eli, that great priest of God, died in heartbreak and shame because, as the Word of God says, "...his sons made themselves vile, and he restrained them not." Spiritual training is incomplete and inadequate if it does not include the practical applications such as requiring instant obedience, respect for parents, a love for work, honesty, cheerfulness, etc. Shame on us, Christians, if we give the world an opportunity to sneer at our "spirituality" because of what they see in our children!

"Train up a child in the way he should go: and when he is old, he will not depart from it."--Prov. 22:6.

HURRY! HURRY! HURRY!

Yesterday, in the middle of a last minute rush for an appointment, my little girl said to me, "Mommy, why do we always have to hurry? You are always saying, 'Let's hurry and get our clothes on' and 'Let's hurry and finish our cereal.' Why DO we always have to hurry?"

I told her (a little defensively) that children had shorter legs and arms and were smaller all over and that sometimes they had to move a little bit faster to keep up with big people. But the guilty thought struck me that really it would be much more logical to expect grown people to work a little harder at slowing down for the children.

Isn't it funny that we spend half a lifetime trying to learn to do things fast and "efficiently" and then suddenly when we have children we have to learn that often the slow way with children is the efficient way? For instance, have you ever tried to comb a little girl's long hair when you were in a hurry? The results are painful for the child and quite discouraging for the mother! The faster you comb the harder it pulls, the more the child squirms and the tighter become the snarls!

I've discovered that getting children ready for bed goes much faster if we don't rush it too much. If I bathe my children hurriedly, get them into their pajamas fast, leave out the bedtime story and send them to bed with just a brief prayer, they are restless and unsatisfied and have a hard time getting to sleep. They find all kinds of excuses to call me back into the room--for a drink of water, another goodnight kiss, a blanket that needs to be tucked in. In the long run I save time by taking the whole process at a more leisurely pace. When all is said and done, I think maybe I even feel a little more tender and loving when I am unhurried in getting the children to bed.

Not too long ago I was at a department store counter waiting for a clerk to wrap the merchandise I had just bought. At another counter not far away a hurried mother looked around to find that her little daughter had wandered several feet away. She grabbed her child by the arm with a jerk that almost pulled the little girl off her feet. A man standing nearby mut-

tered angrily, "Women like that oughn't to be allowed to have children." Though I myself thought her treatment to be rather harsh, I was certain that in reality the woman probably loved her girl very much. She was in a hurry; she had something else on her mind. All mothers face the same temptation. In the process of feeding and clothing and training our children we are caught up in the fast-moving machinery of the thing and forget to enjoy the product we're working on! We have a mother's heart; it is just that we have lost our mother's touch.

Isn't it good that the Lord never gets in too big a hurry to be the compassionate, loving, gentle parent which we, His dear children, need? How longsuffering and patient He is with us, no matter how perverse and foolish we are. And how persistently and carefully does the Holy Spirit guide us in our walk and in our training--never in a hurry and never in impatience! I may lose the mother's touch, perhaps even the mother's heart, but our dear Heavenly Parent never will!

"Can a woman forget her sucking child, that she should not have compassion on the son of her womb? yea, they may forget, yet will I not forget thee."--Isa. 49:15.

"But thou, O Lord, art a God full of compassion, and gracious, longsuffering, and plenteous in mercy and truth."--Ps. 86:15.

A Knight in Shining Armour

Isn't June a lovely time of year? Depending on your viewpoint, it may mean summer vacation, perhaps, or graduation, or gardening, or picnics, or travel or--most exciting of all--weddings! I get a special warm feeling every time a wedding announcement appears in the mail; and we've had several already this spring. Even as formal as wedding announcements are, they have a way of showing the taste and characteristics of the bride and groom. Marcella and Al, for instance (who by the time you read this will be happily honeymooning, God willing), included in their invitation a small card which read:

"We rejoice to invite you to the second greatest event of our natural lives . . . our wedding. The greatest event, however, was our personal conversion to Jesus Christ. We trust that you, too, have experienced this salvation by faith in Him, and will join us at the marriage feast of the Lamb."

Bonnie and Bill, friends from Pontiac, Michigan, surprised us by appearing at our house for coffee the day BEFORE we received an announcement saying they had been married the previous Saturday!

Regardless of how different the bride and groom, the romance, the announcement or the ceremony, each marriage carries with it that hope and dream that the new relationship will bring a fulfillment of the richest joys life has to offer. The most amazing thing of all is that one's ideas of what marriage ought to hold begin to be formed almost as soon as life begins.

Can you still recall the girlhood image you had of the knight in shining armour with whom you would some day live happily ever after? My impressions are still very clear of the "ideal husband" I pictured as a girl. His physical characteristics were never quite jelled in my mind. Sometimes he was blond and blue-eyed; sometimes he was dark. I was positive, however, about the rest. He was a composite of all the best things I had ever known or read about good men. He bore some characteristics of my own beloved dad as well as the heroes of a dozen favorite novels. Sometimes I could see

his image faintly in a choice school friend and always there was a resemblance to some great and famous man out of a history book. My prince charming, I was certain, would be wise and good, bold and yet tender, practical and yet artistic, creative and brilliant and humble and gentle and loving--all rolled into one man. It never occurred to me that there was the slightest contradiction of personality! (At the risk of sounding smug, let me add that the man I married has matched my "ideal" more fully than I would have dared to think possible.)

Maturity and experience and a little heart-break do add a reality to one's dreams. And that is good. Still, I find I resent the philosophy which assumes that high, idealistic standards are not important in choosing a life partner, only the fact of whether or not one is in love. I have heard young girls say about a doubtful friendship, "Well, maybe he does drink (or smoke, or swear, etc); he loves me so much that I'm certain I can get him to stop after we're married." Unfortunately, love is not enough when it is not based on character and integrity. Almost any woman who ever married, hoping to reform a man, will tell you that spiritual and moral problems are usually made worse, rather than better, by the union.

I once heard a lovely Chinese girl insist firmly that romantic love ought to be the out-come of a good marriage, not the preliminary requisite. She said that her mother and father had--in the best oriental tradition--been given to each other in marriage through no decision of their own. They had not chosen each other, but because they loved the Lord and had been carefully reared, they learned to love each oth-er deeply and tenderly AFTER they were mar-ried.

Well, regardless of how romantic two people feel when they marry, love does sometimes get a little tarnished from neglect or scratched from mistreatment. Like good silver, it ought to be enjoyed and used everyday, and polished often! The best formula for "love polish" I know anything about is found in Ephesians 4, verses 30-32 (the same book, incidentally, which com-mands us rather pointedly, "Wives, submit yourselves unto your own husbands, as unto the Lord"):

"And grieve not the holy Spirit of God, where-

by ye are sealed unto the day of redemption. Let all bitterness, and wrath, and anger, and clamour, and evil speaking, be put away from you, with all malice: And be ye kind one to another, tenderhearted, forgiving one another, even as God for Christ's sake hath forgiven you."

A Woman's Work Is Never Done

I'm sure I don't have to convince you that the old cliche, "A woman's work is never done," however tiresome, is nevertheless true. When my kitchen floor is scrubbed and polished to a gleaming mirror (a rare and delightful sight!) I nurse a private hope that it will stay that way at least a week. Every housewife knows that the wastepaper baskets, now freshly emptied, will fill up again. The dishes, just washed and put away, will soon be sticky again with egg or gravy or pudding. The beds, sweet-smelling with clean linens, will soon be rumpled and undone. And of course the very moment you are taking pride in the fact that the ironing is done right down to the last handkerchief, a pair of little boys' pants will be getting muddy, a tablecloth will be getting soiled and a father's white shirt will be hitting the hamper. Some jobs last a little longer than a week or a month and they are the ones most of us really enjoy seeing finished--cleaning woodwork or shampooing the rugs or washing curtains. The traditionally annual jobs such as painting or refinishing walls and furniture and cleaning the drapes bring the most completely satisfying feeling of all.

Once in a while at our house things go so awry that the work gets undone even before it is really done. Right in the middle of waxing the floor I stop to answer the phone, and while I am talking, several small pairs of muddy feet come tracking right through the wet wax. Or if I am late washing up the dinner dishes there is unexpected company, so I leave the dishes in the water and put on a pot of coffee and we start the dirty-dish cycle over again before the last is even completed! Though the fault often lies with bad planning or poor timing, there are days when, in spite of all my best efforts, absolutely nothing goes right. By the time Don gets home at night the children are tired and cranky, I am tearful and frustrated, and dinner is still in the refrigerator.

Occasionally the same thing happens in the Lord's work. You leave for Sunday School with exactly enough time to pick up the two families of children who have promised to come with you. At the first house the children are not dressed, and so you have to wait. By the time

103

you get to the second house, the people have gotten discouraged waiting, and finally deciding you had forgotten, have sent their children off for a picnic with a friend. Naturally you arrive at Sunday School late, breathless, disappointed and disorganized.

Or perhaps you plan a party for a Sunday School class of 12-year-old girls. The refreshments are prepared, the games are planned, your home schedule has been rearranged so that the party will go smoothly. At the last minute one little girl arrives who explains that the other girls are "mad" at her about something and have therefore decided not to come.

On just such frustrating occasions the first verse from Psalm 127 forces its way rather pointedly into my mind: "Except the Lord build the house, they labour in vain that build it: except the Lord keep the city, the watchman waketh but in vain." Regardless of what we are "building," regardless of its importance or worth, either in our home life or for the cause of Christ, if we do not seek the Lord's blessing and power, we "labour in vain that build." Even housework is prospered and made effective when we ask the Lord to make it so. How

much more true, then, that the Lord's work, done in His way and with His power, will bring forth fruit and blessing.

Just this week Mrs. Jack Hyles, a busy mother and wife of an outstanding soul-winning pastor, reminded me of the prayer in Psalm 90:17 which I have since decided to make my own daily petition:

"And let the beauty of the Lord our God be upon us: and establish thou (or 'make good') the work of our hands upon us; yea, the work of our hands establish thou it."

Home Is Where the Heart Is

One evening last week I stood in the middle of an ordinary parking lot on an ordinary street and tried hard to swallow the sudden lump that had come to my throat. To the casual observer there was certainly nothing special about the scene, but to me it represented something precious.

Not too many years ago that parking lot had been the site of an old rambling house which had, sometime in its long history, been divided into a number of rather makeshift apartments. One of those apartments, perhaps the most makeshift one of all, was Don's and my first home.

As I stood there I had to fight down a feeling of something akin to resentment that so many people should so absent-mindedly drive their cars over the graveled surface of a lot which to me held all the dear and sacred memories of home. Of course they had no reason to remember the view from our single kitchen window of the huge willow tree, or the smell of lilacs there in the early spring, nor had they known the love and laughter--and the tears, too--which had made that old house a home. A room is just a room, an apartment is just an apartment, a house is just a house unless it is YOUR room or apartment or house--then it is HOME.

It is hard to describe the essence of what a home is. Perhaps it is first and foremost the place where one's possessions are--whether physical or spiritual. Don and I have traveled many times between Moline, Illinois, and Wheaton, Illinois. We have lived in both places, have friends and family in both places and so both cities are dear to our hearts. When we were living in Moline we loved to visit all our family and friends in Wheaton, but there was always a certain restful pleasure in going back "home" to Moline. Now that we are living in Wheaton, we look forward to every visit with our loved ones in Moline, but we always enjoy coming back "home" to Wheaton. In spite of the fact that there are many we love in both places, home is still the place where our possessions lie.

When I was in high school I had a wonderful English teacher, Miss Ruby Lindblad, who had formerly been a missionary to India. She once told us an incident of her life which has made a lasting impression on mine. While she was in India she contracted a disease which the doctor diagnosed as being incurable and so she was sent home to America to die. At first she was almost overwhelmed at the thought of her approaching death, but day by day she grew more and more used to the idea. Before long her heart became so prepared for Home-going that she found herself longing for the hour when she would see her Saviour. When she woke up in the morning she would think, "Perhaps this will be the day!" When she went to sleep at night her last thought would be, "Perhaps tonight He will call me Home!" She said that her anticipation was like that of a bride longing to see her bridegroom away in a far country.

As sometimes happens in the providence of God, Miss Lindblad's incurable disease proved to be "curable" and the day came when the amazed doctors pronounced her well. Then came the most difficult adjustment of all. The shock of facing the fact that she would not live was nothing to facing the disappointment that Heaven and Home were not as near as she had

believed. She had so transferred her heart and possessions and longings to that other shore, that the world had become in reality an alien land.

Does Heaven seem far away and remote? Or is there a longing that compels us to be quick about doing our Father's business, in the joyful anticipation that perhaps today He will call us Home, or come for us in the sky?

"Lay not up for yourselves treasures upon earth, where moth and rust doth corrupt, and where thieves break through and steal: But lay up for yourselves treasures in heaven, where neither moth nor rust doth corrupt, and where thieves do not break through nor steal: For where your treasure is, there will your heart be also."--Matt. 6:19-21.

"What's in a Name?"

One of the great rewards of having a large host of relatives is that there is always something happening. One never has a chance to sit back with a "ho-hum" and ponder over how boring life can become. There is always a new baby, a wedding, an operation, a new home or some special advancement for someone in the family! And when one's family is especially close, the joys and excitements and heartaches are even more completely shared.

Right now we are at a temporary standstill as far as family weddings are concerned. My youngest sister was married last August and all the nieces and nephews in the family are still a little young to be starting anything exciting in that direction. That makes our most current and frequent interest a rather regular parade of new babies. Libby and Walt, who already had five lovely boys and girls, have just added a precious set of twins to their little hoard and now this morning Joanna and Bill became parents of their third child and first boy--John Robert Rice. Early in the fall we will all be looking forward to the arrival of Joy's first baby. So, as I said, babies have become our most frequent topic of conversation!

With nineteen various and assorted cousins on one side of the family alone, it has become increasingly difficult to find just the right name for each new baby. In spite of our best efforts, some of the names get repeated here and there and we have to distinguish between cousins by adding a second name. The problem is even greater when two little ones have to be named at the same time. The little Handford twins went around for several days as "little boy" and "little girl" before they became perfectly and permanently labeled as Billy and Judy, or more properly, William Lee and Judith Ann.

Don and I have always tried to have some special significance in the names we gave our babies. Each of our children carries the name of someone dear, but at the same time we have tried to make the combination of names simple and pleasing in sound. We have pretty much come to the conclusion that the classical, traditional names, however common, seem to wear better than the unusual ones. Modern, faddish names, though often "cute," have always bothered me a little, especially when I have considered how they will sound addressed to a full-grown man or woman. Of course the reverse is true also. A long, pompous family name can sound mighty awkward and out-of-place on a little pink-cheeked, fuzzy-headed baby!

Well, regardless of the given name, it is the surname which finds a place of utmost importance in society. The rights of an heir belong to the child who bears his father's name. And with the rights go a number of responsibilities.

I read recently that Caroline Kennedy, daughter of the President, is often stopped short in the middle of tears by the reminder, "Kennedy's don't cry." I'm not exactly sure WHY Kennedy's don't cry, but at least a little girl is learning to respect the standards of the family name she wears. I have heard my father say that when he was a boy growing up, his father would frequently remind him, "Son, remember you are a Rice." Often that was all that was needed to keep him from some special temptation to do wrong.

There ought to be a sense of honor that accompanies a family name. And what is true on

a human level is certainly true on a spiritual level as well. As a human father takes pride in a son which brings him honor, so the Lord delights in His children who bring glory to His name. Take the case of Job, for example. How pleased the Lord must have been when He said to Satan, "Hast thou considered . . . Job, that there is none like him in the earth, a perfect and an upright man . . .?" And in the same sense that an earthly father loves and pleads with a wayward son, so the Lord tenderly pleads with His backslidden children:

"If my people, which are called BY MY NAME, shall humble themselves, and pray, and seek my face, and turn from their wicked ways; then will I hear from heaven, and will forgive their sin, and will heal their land."--II Chron. 7:14.

What an awesome responsibility that our Heavenly Father, just as certainly and completely as any earthly father,' calls us by His name'!

Fudgie-Budgies

It was one of those mornings.

Everybody woke up complaining and feeling out of sorts. Carol wished I had fixed cereal instead of eggs for breakfast. Donnie was fussy; he didn't want to eat anything. Jimmy was pouting because he had to wear play clothes instead of Sunday clothes. Both of the big children wanted to drink their orange juice out of the blue plastic glass instead of their usual pink and yellow ones. Nothing looked right, tasted right, or felt right to any of the children. Finally, in exasperation, I said, "Now look, we've got a whole house full of fuss-budgets this morning. Let's see if we can't be happy and nice the rest of the day."

By noon the world looked much brighter. When we sat down to lunch Carol said, "Mommy, were we good this morning, or were we fudgie-budgies?" I took a quick sip of soup to hide my snicker and then told her that it looked like our fudgie-budgies had turned out to be pretty nice boys and girls after all.

Some people are chronic complainers. But occasionally, only too rarely, you meet a person who is constantly cheerful and optimistic. My husband's 91-year-old grandmother is just such a person. In the shattering experience of transplanting her family from her beloved Sweden to America, in the sorrow of losing two children and a husband by death, through years of hard work and sacrifice she has never lost her gentle, uncomplaining spirit. She is pleased and grateful at every gesture of kindness, never requiring any time or attention more than what people are able to give her.

Just a couple of weeks ago Grandma Sandberg fell and broke her hip. After an hour-long ride to the hospital in an ambulance, she went through all the discomforts of such an injury without a whisper of complaint--X-rays, shots, blood pressure readings, tests of every description and finally, surgery. She never let a nurse leave the room after administering a pill or a shot without saying, "Thank you." And because she is old and forgetful, she would sometimes say "thank you" again just in case she had forgotten the first time! It is not hard to understand why everyone in the hospital fell in love with her. Grateful, cheerful people are just plain nice to be around.

The world is full of fudgie-budgies--chronic complainers. The weather is never right for fudgie-budgies. They always feel misunderstood by their friends and mistreated by their families. They are always quite certain that all the joys and privileges of life have been handed out to other people. They are always so absorbed in the thoughtlessness and selfishness of others that they completely miss the smiles and kindnesses of those who love them. Indeed, they often convince themselves that no one does love them. How sad it is to be a fudgie-budgie!

Christians, of all people, have no business becoming chronic complainers. How wonderful to have all the blessings of life eternal; perfect and immediate access to the throne of an Almighty, all-loving God, a sympathetic Friend to share every burden and finally, the blessed hope of a home in Heaven where "sorrow and sighing shall flee away."

Tell me, are you a fudgie-budgie?

"Occupy Until I Come"

What a busy week this has been! Now that school is over my big job is getting the whole family ready for a summer of camp work. The last of the winter clothes have to be cleaned and put away; summer things have to be sorted, lengthened and mended. Play shoes have to be bought and summer play equipment has to be located. There are camp activities to be planned and handcraft work to be prepared. And then the biggest job of all is that of getting the house in order for my sister Joy and her husband Roger to live in while we are away.

Have you ever tried to get your house ready for someone else to occupy--even for a few days? It is rather an eye-opening experience. Even after a thorough cleaning is done (if it gets done)--things don't seem quite right. In the familiar routine of everyday life, we get where we don't even really "see" our home. It seems pleasantly comfortable and familiar until we begin to picture it through the eyes of an outsider. Then suddenly everything looks a little shabbier than usual. The upholstery on our favorite rocking chair is becoming embarrassingly worn. The kitchen curtains are definitely showing a need of replacement. And we can't pretend any longer that the odd assortment of furniture in the children's rooms has anything to do with good taste!

Most of these defects are apparent even when one is expecting company for an evening. But the point at which I really begin to feel exposed is when I realize that someone will be looking under the sink for the dishpan, brushing teeth in my bathroom and hanging clothes in my closet. Then I am forced to survey the condition of my cupboards, closets and drawers. All at once I feel the urge to systematize all the little hidden recesses of my home which are not usually subject to the scrutiny of other people.

Of course Joy and Roger are really "family" and are not likely to be especially critical, but still one likes to appear well organized even to familiar friends and family. Chances are, however, that even having known what the deadline was for several months everything won't get done before Joy and Roger move in. I'm sure the rocking chair won't be re-covered, the kitchen curtains won't be made, and probably a good many other things will be left undone beside.

Just think how much more embarrassing it is going to be when the Lord comes and finds our "heart house" in sad need of cleaning and repair! It is one thing to keep the living room in order for casual company, but it is quite another thing to have every secret corner, every private drawer and closet thrown open for public inspection! Some of us who pride ourselves on the kind of housekeeping we do in our homes have all sorts of dirty, cluttered corners in our hearts. We don't intend to leave them that way; we tell ourselves that surely there will be time to get things in order before the Guest arrives. It's just that the deadline seems so far away. I wonder how many of us will be caught with sin lurking in some hidden closet where we hoped no one would ever find it?

"But of the times and the seasons, brethren, ye have no need that I write unto you. For yourselves know perfectly that the day of the Lord so cometh as a thief in the night. For when they shall say, Peace and safety; then sudden destruction cometh upon them, as travail upon a woman with child; and they shall not escape. But ye, brethren, are not in darkness, that that day should overtake you as a thief . . . . Therefore let us not sleep, as do others; but let us watch and be sober." -- II Thess. 5:1-3, 5.

Summer Fruit

As far as I'm concerned, summer is really here when I taste that first batch of rhubarb sauce--pink and tart and wonderfully delicious. From then on I can hardly wait for all the other fruits and vegetables that summer brings--zucchini squash, garden tomatoes, tender sweet corn right from the field, strawberries, melons, green beans and fresh asparagus. I am not one to turn up my nose at the amazing array of frozen foods one can buy at the grocery store, but I'll have to admit that nothing from a frozen food locker can taste quite so good as the fruits and vegetables fresh out of a summer garden. My mouth waters at the thought!

Since we are to be away from home all summer long we didn't put in a garden. However, I do have one little strawberry patch which is doing beautifully. Last year the birds beat me to every single ripe red berry and I had determined that this year I would get the best of them. I have strung up bits of shiny aluminum over the plants so that the tinkle and the shimmer will scare them away, and so far I've got them fooled. How much fun it has been to bring in a big handful of strawberries every day!

At our house, we have a special fancy for fresh tomatoes--especially the meaty, beefsteak variety. One year I was so hungry for them I decided I was really going to eat my fill. I almost hoped I would get just a little bit tired of them so that when fall came, I wouldn't mind so much not having them. We ate them in salads, put them in sandwiches, stewed them and stuffed them with cottage cheese. (Really, though, tomatoes taste best when eaten warm right from the garden with a salt shaker nearby!) That summer we had tomatoes at our house for nearly every meal and often for snacks in between. But even with all that indulging, I felt a pang of regret when the first frost brought an end to the summer crop.

Every season, of course, has its own store of special delicacies and treats. In the fall we have crisp new apples and squash and pumpkin. In the winter there are wonderful citrus fruits. In the spring there are a few early berries and fruits and then we begin the round of seasons all over again. We always feel a little bad when one type of food is out of season but our loving Heavenly Father always sees to it that there is something else good to take its place.

Some of you are probably familiar with the old hymn which says:

**"Thy Word is like a garden, Lord,
with flowers bright and fair
And every one who seeks may pluck
a lovely cluster there."**

It is true that many parts of the Bible are fragrant and beautiful as flowers, but I take a great deal of delight in picturing it rather as an inexhaustible fruit and vegetable garden. Flowers are to be looked at, smelled and admired--but their usefulness ends there. Food is to be enjoyed not merely for its beauty and fragrance, but especially because it pleases the taste and satisfies the appetite. When the spiritual appetite has not been spoiled by indulgence in the wrong kind of food, the Word of God supplies all kinds of rich and sweet morsels to satisfy every taste and every possible kind of heart hunger.

Most blessed fact of all--the Word of God has no seasons. Whether the heart is wrapped in the cold of winter or is warm with the sunshine of summer, the Bible is always at the peak of season. There is no frost to cut off a perfect summer crop and there is no such thing as the end of the harvest. The more the fruit is plucked, the more abundantly it grows. The quality of the fruit is never damaged by the hailstorms of skeptics or by the worms of apostasy. There is always food--sufficient for every appetite, varied for every taste--just for the taking.

"Thy words were found, and I did eat them, and thy word was unto me the joy and rejoicing of mine heart: for I am called by thy name, O Lord God of hosts."--Jer. 15:16.

Allana Jean

I wish you could know my tiny little niece, Allana Jean. She was adopted by Grace and Allan when just a few weeks old and she won our hearts immediately by her elfin proportions and her winsome ways. Now that she is two and a half she is still petite and graceful and dainty as a flower.

Allana wins friends wherever she goes. She has a way of fluttering dark eyes in a fashion that would melt the heart of marble! And her honey-rose complexion would be the envy of any girl. Sometimes Allana wears curls--that is, when her natural girlish vanity can win over her insatiable curiosity as to what makes curlers go up and what makes curlers come down! When her mother gets discouraged with the soft brown hair from which the curlers have been repeatedly removed, then Allana wears her hair in a spritely little pony-tail that goes straight up in back.

Allana's most charming attribute is her expressive personality. When she is unhappy,

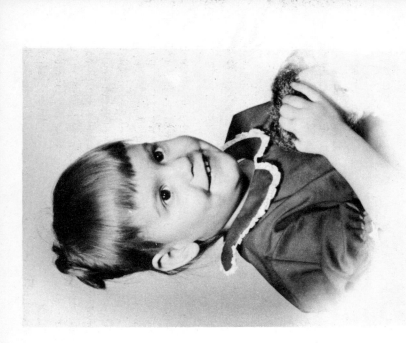

she wears a look of tragedy that would be the envy of any Shakespearean actor. When she is tired, she huddles in a little heap with two small fingers in her mouth. But when she is happy, it is springtime and Christmas and happy-birthday all rolled into one! At one moment she may be sailing through the house like a fairy and the next moment she is clomping back in the clownish gait of a dancing bear, all the while squealing with delight at herself and the world.

She is a wondrous mixture of curiosity, tenderness, mischief and sageness so peculiar to children of intense personality. The mother-instinct is already so strong in her that she is almost transfixed in the presence of babies. She will spend an unbelievable amount of time gently fondling them, bringing them bits of cookies (or whatever other food she can find), taking off their shoes, playing with their hair, etc.

At times Allana becomes a little executive, minding everybody's business. If big brother David is doing something he ought not to be doing, she either straightens him out herself or runs to get mother. She likes to get a Kleenex when another child has a runny nose and makes quite a show of "tying" loose shoelaces of the other children.

Allana's awareness of life is especially surprising in light of the fact that she cannot hear. She does not know what it is to hear a mother's tender whisper, the lilting song of a bird, the gurgle of a baby. Some sounds come through to her, like the resonant beat of a drum, a whistle, a deep-throated horn and then her face lights up with the most thrilling look of wonder.

Soon Allana will be fitted with a special hearing-aid. There will be training and more training and more training. With the combination of patient teaching and scientific equipment, coupled with Allana's own natural acuteness, we expect her, by God's mercy, to have a wonderfully happy, normal life of great usefulness.

There is a state of deafness much sadder than Allana's and that is a deafness to the tender, pleading voice of God. Can it be that the Lord has been talking to YOU about something --a cherished habit, a secret sin, a love of pleasure or possessions, a coldness to His Word?

When I was a child, my sisters and I were expected to come when called. The excuse "I didn't hear," would never do. We were reminded that it was our business to be always listening for the sound of Mother or Dad's voice. Perhaps we, like careless children, have been turning a deaf ear to the call of God. Let us turn quickly and say, like Samuel, "Speak, Lord, for thy servant heareth."

"Observe and HEAR all these words which I command thee, that it may go well with thee, and with thy children after thee for ever, when thou doest that which is good and right in the sight of the Lord thy God."--Deut. 12:28.

Pots and Pans

Some have said that you can tell the quality of a cook by looking at her pots and pans. I'm not too certain what conditions a judge would look for--whether quantity of cookware, quality, cleanliness or what-have-you. An expert cookie-maker I know says that cooky sheets have to be kept to a shining polish if you want to make sure your cookies always come out just right. On the other hand, some kitchen utensils do better, I am told, if they are kept away from water. For instance, some people insist that fried eggs, to be cooked to perfection, ought to be fried in a big, black cast-iron skillet which is never washed, merely wiped clean after each use. My husband says his grandmother would never let her breadpans be put in the dishpan because it would make the bread stick. They, too, were wiped clean and put away, never to be used for anything except for baking bread.

I have such a motley assortment of pots and pans that I am certain they would prove nothing except that I am a rather disorganized housewife! There are copper-bottom pans which require a bit of polishing now and then, a few stainless steel, and then a peculiar collection of other cooking utensils which boast no kinship either to themselves or the others!

When I was first married I especially enjoyed my shiny new copper-bottom pans. I had a rack up so that they could be prominently displayed. Of course that meant they had to be polished every time they were used, but I was a bride and every part of housekeeping was still very exciting, so I didn't object a bit. However, I did discover one sad truth about copper-bottom pans: they heat up very fast, and unless one watches them very closely there will be burned potatoes for dinner! After seven years of marriage I find my copper pans still outwit me all too frequently.

One pan which gets a great deal of use at my house is the pressure-saucepan. I never get over the wonder that inexpensive meats can be cooked quickly and come out tender and delicious through the magic of the pressure cooker. When time is at a premium, I find the cooker is wonderful for getting almost anything done in a hurry--potatoes, vegetables, beans, apple-sauce. Here again, the problem is that I must watch the pressure cooker rather closely. If the pressure is not adjusted properly, or if the right amount of water is not used, then there is a danger of blowing the safety valve. (I've had it happen. Though the experience is harmless enough, the noise it makes and the inconvenience of replacing the part makes one want to avoid letting it happen twice!)

When all is said and done, the pan which gets the most use at my house is the smallest and humblest of all. It is not shiny and it certainly is not expensive. In fact, it does not even claim a matching lid. It is rarely used in making company meals and it never makes an appearance at the table like some of the fancier, modern "cook and serve" utensils. Still, it is the pan most seen on the top of my stove. It is the pan that warms the bottles and the baby food. It cooks the soft-boiled eggs every morning and warms up the leftovers. It is easy to clean. Its main virtue is that it is small and unobtrusive enough to keep on the back of the stove most of the time, and it is always ready for any little job I need to use it for. It has no

fancy gadgets; it is not beautiful. It is faithful.

"But in a great house there are not only vessels of gold and of silver, but also of wood and of earth; and some to honour, and some to dishonour. If a man therefore purge himself from these [iniquities], he shall be a vessel unto honour, sanctified, and meet for the master's use, and prepared unto every good work." -- II Tim. 2:20, 21.

Let's Indoctrinate Our Children!

Not too many weeks ago a teacher in one of the nearby high schools was suspended on the charge that he had propagated communism in the public schools. The complaint had been made by several parents that their children had come home from school with the news that their teacher had told them the "good" side of communism. In his own defense the teacher said, "I am not a communist and I have never been one. I feel that it is my duty as a teacher to present both sides of every issue."

On the surface, "to present both sides" sounds innocent enough; in fact, it has a rather noble ring to it. Modern society has made broad-mindedness the supreme virtue. We have been so busy being tolerant, unbiased, non-sectarian and ecumenical that we have almost thrown away the God-given privilege--no, I should say God-given RESPONSIBILITY--of influence over our children. We say, in essence, to the world,

"I'll give you the same opportunities for indoctrinating my children for evil as I give myself to indoctrinate them for good. May the best man win!"

I frequently hear a parent say, "Well, I think young people need to learn to decide for themselves." Baloney! Do children need to decide for themselves that sin does not pay; that there is a Hell and a Heaven; that the Bible is the verbally inspired, inerrant Word of God; that any political system or church system which does not allow for Jesus Christ as the only Redeemer from sin is of the Devil? The truth of the matter is that we are afraid to tell our children that right is always right and wrong is always wrong without any IFS, ANDS, or BUTS. We have concentrated so long on "being acceptable" to everyone that we've lost all our convictions.

When we are teaching young children to stay out of the street, we do not describe to them all the advantages of playing in the street in an effort to give "both sides." If it is dangerous to their health and life, then there are no advantages, no "good points" about playing in the street. It is as simple as that. How strange

119

that we are inclined to be more careless with their spiritual welfare than we are with their bodies.

Why is it that we are all so afraid of the word "indoctrinate"? Throughout the world the communists, the socialists, the Catholics and a thousand other sects and political systems are indoctrinating their youth unashamedly with their doctrines and philosophies. Meanwhile, we evangelical Christians are so absorbed with being broadminded that we allow our children to be exposed to an almost unbelievable number of philosophies and heresies specifically designed to destroy their moral fiber and tear down their faith. The communists know the power of influence and indoctrination. They screen as carefully as possible every bit of information that comes beyond the iron curtain. The Catholic church forbids its constituents to attend any religious services except their own.

We Christians are not so careful. We give our children a slight smattering of spiritual training in the home and in the Sunday School, then we leave it up to the movies, the television, the cheap magazine, the evolution-teaching professor, and the worldly, popular crowd at school to do their worst without ever a word raised in protest. God forgive us!

Dressmaking

I suppose that if I ever had to choose one particular homemaking art as my favorite, it would be dressmaking. There is just something about a wide spread of lovely fabric that makes my fingers itch for a pattern and a pair of scissors. The exciting thing about sewing is that the completed garment is always one of a kind. No matter how common the pattern or the material or the special trim and buttons, the combination makes it completely original.

Sometimes even when the same pattern and material are used to make several garments, the results are not identical. Last Christmas several ladies of the church made little angel costumes for the primary children to wear in the Christmas program. The pattern was a simple T-shaped arrangement without any extra adornment except for a bit of tinsel at the waist, but somehow each costume made by a different lady had a slightly different look about it. Perhaps the difference was in the type of seam used or maybe some of the seamstresses added gussets, but the individuality was there--whatever the reason.

My husband usually picks out the material and the pattern anytime I get ready to make a dress. I trust his taste a great deal more than I do my own. Men seem to have a better eye for that sort of thing. Or perhaps their taste is less influenced by current fads of fashion and so they are more apt judges of basic, long-lasting style. For many years before I was married--and several afterward--my dad picked out nine dresses every Christmas--one for my mother, one each for Miss Viola Walden and Miss Fairy Shappard (who are practically my sisters, having worked at the Sword office for more than 25 years), and one for each of his six daughters. The fit for each was nearly always perfect and the style always just right for each individual "girl." One saleslady in a Wheaton store still tells me how amazed she was at Dad's excellent taste.

When I do my own picking out of materials and patterns I sometimes find that I have chosen a pattern which looked pretty enough on paper but which is really not suited to the fabric at all. I have in my closet a dress which I made

121

seven years ago. The sturdy material is still in excellent condition and the handwork is not too bad. But I wear it rarely, never with real comfort and pleasure. The pattern just did not suit the material. The fabric is too heavy for the flounciness of the skirt and for the cut of the sleeves. I always think that someday I will make it over but of course it always takes a great deal more character to take apart a dress and make it over than it does to start from scratch. I suppose I ought to just give the dress away and be done with it.

Can it be that some of us are like that old dress hanging in the back of my closet? The Lord has given us good material to work with but we have cut our lives to patterns that do not fit the fabric. Perhaps the Lord had a good, practical pattern for us, but we wanted to go by our own design and adorn the garment with little glittering, selfish interests here and there. The result is that we are ill-fitting and uncomfortable garments. Our fabric was designed for usefulness and serviceability, but we have cut the pattern to include so many cumbersome frills and flounces that we are out of place at the kitchen sink of service and dedication. Nor

are we quite at home at the world's riotous parties either. It is no wonder that we spend most of our wasted lives in some back closet of uselessness.

What kind of a pattern have you used for your life? The wrong one? Well, perhaps it is not too late to find some service yet. Let us ask the Lord for the grace to take things apart here and there (and to do a little re-cutting, if necessary) and to make of our lives garments fit for His service.

"I beseech you therefore, brethren, by the mercies of God, that ye present your bodies a living sacrifice, holy, acceptable unto God which is your reasonable service. And be not conformed to this world: but be ye transformed by the renewing of your mind, that ye may prove what is that good, and acceptable, and perfect will of God."--Rom. 12:1, 2.

Staying at Home

The other day I stood at the window and watched eighteen children of various sizes busily playing on our cement-floored carport. Some were riding tricycles, some were playing a tag game, a couple were playing with a toy firetruck, and some were just watching. It made me a little nostalgic for my childhood days when there were nearly always twenty-five or so children collected in our yard or in the vacant lot next door.

It was no accident that there were always a great many children at the house where I grew up. In the first place, we already had six children who lived there so that was a pretty good beginning to a crowd right there. And then because kids love crowds, the very fact that there were so many children there always drew a few more.

I think, too (if I may say this without being misunderstood), that maybe we had a little more fun at our house than did the average family. We always had some project going. Either

we were building a house up in the Chinaberry tree or we were planning a circus with Olga the goat as our main attraction or we were putting on a play. Besides, Dad had rigged up a home-made swing and seesaw and sandbox and that provided hours of pleasure. Sometimes right at dusk he would string up a light outside so that we could all play "Kick the Can" in the semi-darkness. That was just about as exciting a time as children could find! Most special of all, our parents actually PLAYED with us. I didn't know any other parents on the block who did that, and so I was very proud that I had folks who were still young enough to have fun! For refreshments there was usually a bushel basket of Texas oranges on the back porch to which we and our friends were always welcome.

We were not often allowed to play at the homes of other children and were not ever allowed to run about the neighborhood at will. We were taught the verse in Proverbs 25:17, "Withdraw thy foot from thy neighbour's house; lest he be weary of thee, and so hate thee," and were required to take that Scripture quite literally. I remember that the little girl who lived on the corner had a doll house with real wall-

123

paper and curtains, and I could never understand why my mother wouldn't let me go down
there to play everyday.

Now that I have children of my own, I can
see many good reasons why my folks expected
us to play at our own house. Children are
acutely aware of the standards of the homes
where they play. When they are at my home
they know that certain kinds of talk and certain kinds of play are forbidden. In my yard
I can do something about fighting that gets out
of hand. Most important of all, I can occasionally give a little spiritual training to children
who would have no other way of receiving it. I
never need to worry about whether my children
are getting into someone else's garage or
trampling someone else's flowers. And there
is a distinct advantage in always having my own
children within sight and calling distance.

Of course there are disadvantages to having
a yard full of neighborhood children. One always has to do a little more "babysitting"
where there are more children around, and
then there is always the possibility that tools
and toys will be broken with so many in the
yard. There is always more clutter and more

noise. But what a wonderful way to teach children the joy of hospitality!

I wonder if perhaps one of the greatest con-
tributing causes to juvenile delinquency is that
home is no longer associated with happiness
and companionship? I am certain there is a
breakdown in respect for and obedience to parents in homes where children come to sleep
and occasionally to eat, but who always find
their pleasure somewhere else.

Let's teach our children the joys of staying
at home. It isn't easy. There is such a trend
toward almost feverish social activity outside
the home that even our schools and churches
are caught up in the whirl. It has gotten to be
an almost impossible thing to have the whole
family together for every meal. But what a
blessing for young people to learn that home is
the happiest place in the world!

Family Pets

We don't have any pets at our house, which is really a shame for a family with children who love animals the way ours do. Don has promised the children that when they are old enough to help take care of pets--then we will get a dog. The boys and their daddy would like a Boxer; Carol prefers little dogs. I rather think the men will win. With a houseful of little roughnecks, a nervous little Chihuahua would never feel at home.

I said we have no pets. Actually, I should have said we have no WANTED pets. Occasionally a stray cat decides to settle in the crawl-space under our house to raise a family. It is warm and dry there, and evidently quite a comfortable home. Once two old tomcats went under the house to fight a duel and they got into such a frightful row in the middle of the night that they woke the whole family. They screamed and hissed and knocked each other against the plumbing until we were certain they had torn each other limb from limb. Frankly, we

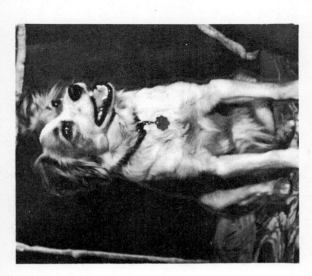

Paw Paw's dog, Flicka

discourage any such stray visitors. It is not that we do not appreciate cats. It is just that the ones who come to see us are not the well-mannered variety. Besides being noisy and of doubtful genealogy, they also bring with them a host of fleas!

125

It is amazing that almost any kind of an animal can become a pet merely because some- one loves it and takes care of it. This spring our four-year-old Carol found a big fat garden worm which she named "Jacob" and carried around very tenderly until I persuaded her that he would really be much happier in the ground. Down the block there is a family who keeps a pet crow. His wings are clipped so that he will not run away and he does a lot of squawking when he is hungry. To the casual observer he seems to be a mean, cantankerous old bird but he is loved by the children who keep him. Also in the neighborhood there is a large white rab- bit which is occasionally exercised by the fam- ily dog, believe it or not. I have seen the dog gently circling the rabbit to keep him close to the house until the little boy who owns both the dog and the rabbit takes his pets into the house.

As I said, a pet has the privileges of home and care and feeding, not necessarily because he is beautiful or expensive, but primarily be- cause he is loved.

My dad has a dog, mostly toy shepherd, named Flicka, who is greatly loved by the whole family. Eleven years ago she joined our

family after she had been thrown from a car window by someone who evidently thought they had too many puppies. She has turned out to be a gentle, sensitive, almost humanly-intelligent dog, though she joined the family without a single credential or recommendation. At first she was loved just because we had adopted her as our own; now of course, she is loved because she has earned that love.

One of the most touching miracles Jesus ever performed was an illustration of the rights and privileges of the family pet. A Syrophenician woman followed Jesus and His disciples, plead- ing that He cast a devil out of her daughter. The self-righteous disciples, who wanted to have nothing to do with her because she was a Gentile, said, "Lord, send her away." To the Jews a Gentile was of no more value than a dog.

Jesus, knowing their hearts and wanting to teach His own disciples a lesson, said, "It is not meet to take the children's bread, and to cast it unto the dogs." One would think she would have been rebuffed at His answer, but she was wise enough to see that He was tender- ly drawing her out.

"Yea, Lord," she answered, "yet the dogs eat

of the crumbs which fall from their masters table."

Jesus must have been moved by her humble profession of faith. Matthew 15:28 ends the story in this way:

"Then Jesus answered and said unto her, O woman, great is thy faith: be it unto thee even as thou wilt. And her daughter was made whole from that very hour."

What a precious privilege that we, whether of the chosen Jewish race, or merely "adopted" into the house of God, have all the blessings of love and care and feeding because we belong to Him. And how rich are the crumbs that fall from the table of the King of kings!

Anybody Hungry?

All summer long I have been enjoying the luxury of sitting down to meals I didn't help prepare, and then leaving the dishes for some-one else to wash! That has been one of the pleasant aspects of spending the summer work-ing with boys and girls at a Christian camp.

Contrary to the general reputation of camp food, ours has been delicious and plentiful. The corn-on-the-cob, fresh garden tomatoes, hot homemade rolls with butter--all have been wonderful. It is amazing how one's appetite increases under the influence of exercise, fresh air and the sight of a hundred or so hun-gry boys and girls sitting down to dinner. Mrs. Freer, the cook, has a way of working magic with the breakfast pancakes and the Sun-day fried chicken, and the crumb cake, too, but even the ordinary cold cereal and Kool-Aid (more commonly known in camp circles as "bug juice") tastes better when served in an atmosphere of laughter and fellowship and sun-shine. Skinny, picky little boys and finicky

127

little girls who won't touch a vegetable at home are sometimes seen at camp gobbling large quantities of canned peas and other commercially prepared vegetables. How many a mother who has sighed and worked over the poor eating habits of her Johnny or Jane would be delighted if she could see how well her children eat at camp.

Of course we work a little at helping the boys and girls to like good food. No matter how much extra money a child brings to camp, he is allowed to spend only a certain amount each day at the snack shack and only at certain specific hours. Younger boys and girls are required to taste a little of each item served in the dining hall whether they think they will like it or not. At the end of each meal every milk glass must be drained right to the bottom.

But aside from the good food and exercise and fresh air, the thing that really makes eating so much fun is that we do it together. The taste of the food is always improved by the laughter and the songs and jokes that always go with a camp meal. Even the worn-out custom of making some counsellor skip around the dining hall to the tune of "The old gray mare; she

ain't what she used to be, etc.," makes mealtime more fun.

I have a great deal of sympathy for people who have to eat all their meals in solitude, or in the company of others who do not enjoy fellowship while they eat. Having meals with people, even little people who often have to be reminded of their manners, must certainly be a great deal more enjoyable than eating alone, with no smiles, no laughter, no pleasant conversation. The best food in the world served on fine china with snowy linen, cut flowers and candlelight, can never be adequate substitute for the joy of happy company at a table of common food.

Occasionally one hears a person claim that he has no need for church attendance or frequent fellowship with other Christians. Such a person usually declares that he can worship God better alone in the beauty of nature or at home while reading or listening to the radio privately, etc., etc., etc. Actually, the spiritual appetite, like the physical appetite, is whetted by the fellowship of others who are hungry. Even carnal Christians, whose tastes have been jaded by a frequent indulgence in the sweets of worldliness, can cultivate a craving for the Living Bread when they see it eaten and enjoyed by hungry-hearted people.

The reverse is true, as well. Christians who think they are so strong that they do not need the constant encouragement and blessing of fellowship with others who love the Lord soon find that they no longer hunger for spiritual food and spiritual fellowship. They become puny, sickly Christians without any appetite for the precious Bread of Life.

Hungry, anyone? Let's eat together!

Leather Carving

One of our projects in the craftshop at Camp Willabay this past summer was leather carving. There were all kinds of leather objects to make --coin purses, wallets, autograph books and picture holders, etc. The first few days of each camp session we had a class in leather carving so that even the children who had never done leatherwork before would know exactly what to do. It was fun to watch the excitement with which the boys and girls started making gifts for all the folks at home.

Most of the children listened very carefully as the instructions were given for dampening the leather and tracing the design to be carved. Those who did nearly always had smiles of pleasure when they saw the design they were about to carve neatly reproduced on the fresh, new slab of leather. Of course there were some who were always in such a hurry to see how everything would turn out that they did not trace slowly enough or carefully enough. They found that they had let the pattern slip so that the design was garbled or incomplete.

Where the design had been carefully copied, the next step--that of actually cutting the design into the leather--was usually not a difficult one. We showed each one exactly how to hold the tool, how deeply to cut, how to cut curves as well as straight edges. When the boys and girls took the time to practice a few strokes before actually cutting into their leather, all went well. Some did not have the skill of the others, and there were mistakes made here and there, but usually the mistakes could be camouflaged with the help of those of us who were teaching.

The next step, which the children always enjoyed most, was that of stamping in the fine design--the background, the delicate centers of the flowers, the veins of the leaves. Occasionally at this point, a child got so excited with all the fascinating shapes and styles of stamping tools at his disposal that he wanted to experiment with them all. He completely disregarded the pattern he was following and filled all the available space on the leather with unrelated symbols. When this happened, the in-

structor, no matter how skilled, usually had a hard time restoring the piece to any kind of usefulness. The child had sacrificed the beauty of the final project for the rather fleeting pleasure of having "tried" everything. I always felt a little sad when this happened--not only because the money and time had been wasted, but because the child had missed the tremendous satisfaction of taking home something which he had made carefully and well, to be praised and admired by his loved ones at home.

What an apt picture of our lives and efforts! Our Heavenly Instructor has given us a perfect design to follow. Sometimes, even when the pattern--traced in the soft impressions of youth

--is garbled, the Lord in mercy takes the carving knife and cuts the design not as it is traced, but as it ought to be. Even the unskilled hand, when guided by His hand, can cut the pattern right. How sad it is when a life, having once been traced and cut to a design of usefulness and blessing, is then wantonly stamped with the symbols of self-will and sin. The pleasure of a little temporary experimenting with sin has irretrievably spoiled the perfect piece. No matter how diligently one attempts to smooth over and blot out and minimize, the damage has been done; the scars will show.

Are you tempted to do a little stamping of your own design today? Wait--follow the pattern--the blessed Word of God!

All About Water

Water is a wonderful substance! Its usefulness is almost unlimited--for quenching thirst, for preparing food, for washing, for lubricating, for cooling, for growing things, for the thousand purposes of industry--water is the universal necessity.

Especially in the heat and dryness of a late summer's day do we realize the preciousness of water. When one has been working hard (or playing hard) on a hot day there is no substitute for a refreshing gulp of cool water or for the splash of it on face and arms. Food often loses its appeal when the weather is extremely warm; even sleep seems somehow less important in summer months, but one's need of water becomes more and more evident as the temperature rises.

In America water has become a symbol of pleasure and relaxation. Waterways which only a few years ago boasted an exclusive summer cottage here and there are now encircled with public beaches and resorts of all kind. Lakes which were once quiet and placid are now studded with boats of every description and their sandy shores are crowded with people vying with each other for a place to sun and swim. For most of us, water is more than a liquid necessary for survival. We associate it with a dozen varied pleasures--the panoramic view of an ocean shoreline perhaps, the tinkle of ice on a hot day, or maybe even the simple pleasure of a warm, sudsy bath.

Water is not always something good and pleasant. Anyone who has seen his home or property destroyed by the ravaging effects of a flood knows that water can be a powerful, frightening thing. A tidal wave which reaches the height of a building several stories high is awesome and terrible. Sometimes even quiet water which appears innocent and pleasant is dangerous.

Not long ago two young friends of ours got very hot and thirsty playing golf. They drank great quantities of the water splashing out of a sprinkling hose which was set up on one of the greens. It looked cool and refreshing and they did not even think to question the purity of the water. After they had already drunk their fill

they discovered to their dismay that the water came from a nearby lake and that it was contaminated. Their violent illness during the following 24 hours gave them opportunity to reflect on the fact that water which looks safe may indeed be very dangerous.

The Bible has a great deal to say about water. In the baptism of the Lord Jesus it symbolized our burial of self and sin; in the washing of the disciples' feet it pictured our daily cleansing from sin. But to me the most blessed scriptural reference to water is that of the woman of Samaria who came to fill her pots with ordinary, earthly water and went away with LIVING water!

Every human heart is thirsty--for peace of heart perhaps, for someone to care, for understanding, for joy, for success in all of life's ventures. And many are thirsty for something which they can't even define. Some have tried tasting the water from the fountains of the world and have found that although the water looks satisfying and refreshing, it is contaminated and brings sickness and trouble in the end.

Are you thirsty today? You may have a drink of the water that satisfies every thirst, every need. Better than that, you may have the fountain within you available for every future need, every future thirst. Just listen to the promise of the Saviour:

"Whosoever drinketh of the water that I shall give him shall never thirst; but the water that I shall give him shall be in him a well of water springing up into everlasting life." --John 4:14.

Self-Discipline

When I was a child I used to be intrigued by the fairy tales in which some individual was granted three wishes. In the stories (as in life) the first heart's desire was usually a foolish one, and so the next two wishes had to be used to correct the problems caused by the fulfillment of the first.

Not long ago I found myself considering what sort of things I would want most for my children if I could choose for them certain special gifts and attributes to make life happy and useful. Of course, all of us who know the Lord would desire first that each of our children would have that most precious gift of all--eternal life. And that ought to be the one single-minded goal of all our training.

But then what? Would we choose for them a brilliant mind? Beauty? Wealth? Fame? A sound body? Unusual talent in music, or speaking ability, or in art? A host of friends? A pleasant personality?

133

I thought over each of those gifts most lauded and sought after by our civilization. What if my children should have wealth without the discipline to use it wisely and well? Wealth could then bring on the direst form of spiritual poverty.

What if my daughter were granted a beauty of face and form without a beauty of character? Is there any ugliness to match the contradiction of a beautiful face over a proud heart?

If my son were granted a brilliant mind without the spiritual perception to weigh humanistic philosophies by the Word of God, what terrible heresy might result.

And how many a young person, gifted with a voice created to move the hearts of millions, has lost the opportunity for blessing he could have had because of a lust for fame and worldly recognition.

Even physical health and strength bring no guarantee of a happy, useful life. If the mind is sick, the emotions immature, then strength of body is no better than that possessed by any jungle animal.

Obviously then, intellect, wealth, beauty, talent, or good health MUST NOT be a parent's

prime desire for his children. Any outstanding human gift or ability without the self-discipline to use it well, is wasted.

In the mercy of God, the reverse is also true. Many a man suffering serious physical or mental handicaps has, through self-discipline, used his very weakness for great blessing. Fanny Crosby's blessed ministry of writing hymns was not IN SPITE OF her blindness but rather BECAUSE of it. Abraham Lincoln's early poverty taught him an appreciation for common men. The Apostle Paul stated that the Lord had given him a greater measure of grace because of his infirmity.

We sometimes conclude, a little illogically, that a person who becomes a Christian should automatically possess a fully-developed, well-built character. We are shocked to discover that a Christian may fall into the grossest type of sin, or that he may seem to be completely lacking in sound moral backbone. But spiritual growth, like physical growth, is not guaranteed just in the process of being born. It is something which must be worked at daily, just as surely as we work at providing for the needs of the body.

Back to the Routine

At last--we are home!

No one would deny that an occasional break in the routine of living is a good thing. Vacations and outings help to refresh our minds and bodies. When our times away from home and regular duties are combined with some kind of service for the Lord, then we are doubly blessed. But after all is said and done, is there any traveling or vacationing which can equal the joy of coming home?

After almost ten long, summer weeks away, our little house seems so pleasantly comfortable and familiar. The old routine of washing dishes, making beds, fixing meals, and scrubbing floors has suddenly become a delightful and fulfilling responsibility. The very "sameness" of the day's schedule brings with it a sense of restfulness after the summer of hectic, exciting activity at camp. And what a relief it is to discipline my children, or kiss my husband, or merely to break into singing any-

What a challenge, then, for all of us who are parents to keep everlastingly at the job of endowing our children with this precious, almost-elusive gift--self-discipline! May God give us wisdom as we teach our children the joy of hard work; the necessity for higher-than-average standards; the responsibility for doing right whether it is easy or hard.

"My son, forget not my law; but let thine heart keep my commandments: For length of days, and long life, and peace, shall they add to thee. . . So shalt thou find favour and good understanding in the sight of God and man."
--Prov. 3:1, 2, 4.

time I like--all in the privacy of my own home! I couldn't help but notice the extra eagerness husband Don felt at getting back to his work-a-day world, too. He actually acted excited when the alarm went off at its regular early hour this morning!

I used to wonder just what the Scripture could possibly mean when it said that God had cursed the ground FOR OUR SAKES. Who would imagine that the hard work which comes with weeds and germs and dirt and disorder could be for our blessing? Most of us would argue that life would certainly be much happier if clothes did not get soiled and worn quite so quickly, and if our work stayed "done" just a little longer. But the Lord in His infinite wisdom and mercy knows that daily, regular toil not only keeps us out of trouble, but it actually makes us happy as well. The very fact that we have to do the same old jobs over and over again provides us with the security of a routine and a purpose.

How inadequate life must seem to people who have no special requirements on their time and efforts. Often a man who has worked regular hours all his life finds that his health and well-being are actually impaired by too much sudden

leisure and lack of routine. Many an older person dies, not because his strength has been used up, but because he no longer has a daily responsibility to make life worth living. Certainly there is an adverse effect on one's emotions and social well-being where there is no schedule or purpose to control daily activities.

I have a brother-in-law who works very hard as a mason contractor. In the heat of summer and cold of winter he keeps busy at the back-breaking job of laying brick and cement block. For many years he dreaded holidays and Sundays because the lack of activity on those days gave him a headache! Perhaps that is the reason he has kept busy on Sundays helping in the young people's meetings or teaching a Sunday School class of exhausting little boys!

Let us then ask the Lord to teach us to delight in a regular routine of daily work and responsibility--not to drag through our labors because we HAVE to do them, but to earnestly, fervently enjoy the everyday duties which are ours.

"Not slothful in business; fervent in spirit; serving the Lord." --Rom. 12:11.

Silly Putty

I wonder if you are familiar with a toy for children which has been on the market for some time now, called "Silly Putty"?

The product is an amazing little blob of stuff which does weird things. If you roll it up in your hands very carefully it will make a ball which will actually bounce. If you pull it like taffy it will break with a brittle-sounding snap. If you merely let it lie it will become a formless, gooey glob! The manufacturers sell the substance with a little plastic container in which it is to be stored. They make a point of encouraging children to keep the putty in its container when not being played with because of the damage it can do if left in the wrong places. Though it keeps firm when being handled, it could easily spoil fine fabrics and rugs if it were left to seep into the fibers. Once, while I was curiously examining "Silly Putty" in a toy department, another mother said to me quite candidly, "If necessary let your children bring mud into the house for amusement, but don't let them play with that stuff. It's too un-predictable. You'll be sorry if you do!"

Some days I feel just like "Silly Putty." If someone rolls me up good at the beginning of the day and gets me going good I can really bounce into the day's work. There is no limit to what I can get done as long as I am "handled" just so. But then if things don't go right or if the pressure of a great deal to do gets a little heavy, then I find I'm ready to snap in two without any warning. Worse yet, if I have nothing to jack me up and get me going, I'm likely to sit around in a useless, uninspired heap, accomplishing nothing. It isn't that I ever intend to spend the day merely marking time; I always plan to really get busy "in just a few minutes" but the longer I sit, the harder it is to pull myself together and get something done. Sometimes my excuse for idleness is tired-ness, or a headache, but just as likely the problem is--purely and simply--a case of laziness.

In all of our churches there is a common problem; never enough people to do the work that needs to be done. If Sunday School classes grew and prospered without much lesson prep-aration, without any visitation or prayer or hard work, then we would all be Sunday School teachers. If a choir could sing melodiously and Spirit-inspired without sacrifice of time and effort and without a willingness to train care-fully regardless of personal glory, then all our churches would have marvelous choirs.

We whimper rather piteously that we do not have enough "trained" or "qualified" workers, but the truth of the matter is that we do not have enough workers who aren't afflicted with laziness. If an exciting new pastor or an en-thusiastic young music director rolls us up and gets us going we bounce along enthusiastically --for awhile. But when the newness of our re-sponsibility begins to wear off, then we either crack at the first disappointment or we give up and sit back and wait for someone with "more training" to do the work we ought to be doing.

Let's not be "Silly Putty." Let's be consci-entious, predictable, dependable workers for the Lord!

"Whatsoever thy hand findeth to do, do it with thy might . . . ."--Eccles. 9:10.

Fenced In!

How fast children grow!

It seems like such a very few months ago that our little Don was a mere baby, content with enjoying life from the confines of a playpen or high chair.

Now everything is different--Donnie can walk! He now regards the playpen as a restricting cage--something to be avoided whenever possi-ble. The high chair, which could once be count-ed on as a safe lodging place for a baby, is now an exciting but dangerous piece of furniture apparently meant for climbing.

The lower kitchen cabinets, the garbage pail, the wastebaskets and the closets are, in Don-nie's eyes, exhaustless treasure coves. What could be more fun than discovering a whole box of paper cups to be chewed, smashed, stacked or sat upon? Food somehow tastes better when salvaged from a garbage pail than it did one hour ago when served properly on a baby's plate! And of course every toddler knows that pots and pans make lots more noise than the rattles and musical toys in the toybox. No wonder babies don't like to be "fenced in"--there are just too many exciting things to try and taste in the big world beyond the bars of the playpen!

Aside from the fact that paper cups cost good money, that garbage is messy when scattered over the kitchen floor, and that the banging of pots and pans will eventually make any mother nervous, there are more important reasons why we do not let our little ones run about at will without any restriction or supervision. All of us know that even the safest homes hold countless dangers for inquisitive little hands and mouths. Of course we want our children to learn to take care of themselves and that naturally involves some experimentation, but we would never want the learning to be at the price of health or well-being.

Not all fences have bars made of wood or iron. Where possible, we move poisons and knives high beyond the reach of little hands. But sometimes dangerous objects cannot or ought not to be moved. In such cases we give the stern command, "Don't touch!" and then, if that command is disobeyed, we enforce it with a spanking which leaves no doubt in a child's mind of the urgency of the command. In many cases good, consistent discipline is a more impenetrable safeguard than any high shelf or locked door.

Titus 2:14 says that Christ came "... that he might redeem us from all iniquity, and purify unto himself a peculiar people, zealous of good works." Five times in the Old Testament God's people are called "a peculiar people." I just recently learned that a literal translation of that word "peculiar" in the Old Testament could be "surrounded," or "enclosed." In other words, we are an encircled people--we are fenced in! The Psalmist David gives the same idea in Psalm 4:3 when he says "... the Lord hath SET APART him that is godly for himself." Then in Psalm 5:12 he adds, "For thou, Lord, wilt bless the righteous; with favour wilt thou COMPASS him as with a shield."

Not only are we restricted from the dangers and consequences of sin by His rebuke (and occasionally by His chastisement), but we are tenderly and lovingly encompassed by His mercy and care. We are set apart and protected just as surely as a careful and loving father would protect an especially beloved child.

What a wonderful thing--to be "fenced in" by the Lord!

Life Is Not Equal

"Jimmy's apple is bigger than mine!"

". . . But Mommy, it isn't my turn to dry the dishes!"

"That isn't fair. Carol got to sit by Daddy last time!"

Is there anything that wears a mother out as much as the struggle to make life equal for her children? Every child is certain that someone else has more privileges, more treats, less work and less supervision than they themselves do. I have even been startled to hear one of my children ask, "Mommy, do you love me as much as you love Baby Don?" And try as hard as one might, there is no way--absolutely no way--a good parent can make everything come out exactly even for each child in the family. Life is just not that way. Even though we may love each of our children enough to give of our very lives for them, we still cannot control the providence which gives one extremely good health and another a sickly body. We cannot insure them an equal share of happiness or worldly goods, no matter how hard we try. The truth of the matter is that God has never intended that any two lives be "equal." When each individual is "custom made," then every circumstance, every human relationship, every opportunity for success, every physical and mental characteristic is part of the master plan for that individual.

When I was in high school I knew a pair of identical twins who were more alike in every way than any two people I've ever seen. Both were lovely girls and very talented. They dressed alike, sang together beautifully and would only date if they could date together! (Since they were both so attractive, they never had trouble finding boy friends who would a-gree to this arrangement.) They even had that strange sixth sense frequently occurring in identical twins which makes one aware of the other's sickness or trouble even though they may be many miles apart. But even for twins, each life has to pursue its own course. Eventually one of the girls had a long seige of illness; the other did not. One twin went to college; the other took a job. Both girls finally married and moved to different parts of the country. With all their similarities of physical characteristics, background and interests, their lives have not been "equal."

It is frequently a problem with Christians that some particular unsaved person who cares nothing at all for God or spiritual things prospers in everything his hand touches. We all sometimes chafe at what seems to be an unfair distribution of life's blessings. Some appear to have more than their share of good health, material wealth, friends and influence, while others are destined to a lifetime of poverty, sorrow and ignobility. We are upset that the pleasures of earth do not come to man in direct and obvious proportion to his virtues and dedication to God.

What a wonderful thing it would be if we could learn to trust in the Omniscient God who holds the balances of life in His own hand! Just think --never to be envious or vexed when others, no matter how unworthy, get fame or wealth or worldly favors--how blessed it would be!

Read again the reassuring 37th Psalm and notice especially the following verses:

"Fret not thyself because of evildoers, neither be thou envious against the workers of iniquity. For they shall soon be cut down like the grass, and wither as the green herb . . . Rest in the Lord, and wait patiently for him: fret not thyself because of him who prospereth in his way, because of the man who bringeth wicked devices to pass . . . For evildoers shall be cut off: but those that wait upon the Lord, they shall inherit the earth. For yet a little while, and the wicked shall not be: yea, thou shalt dili- gently consider his place, and it shall not be. But the meek shall inherit the earth: and shall delight themselves in the abundance of peace. . . . Wait on the Lord, and keep his way, and he shall exalt thee to inherit the land: when the wicked are cut off, thou shalt see it. I have seen the wicked in great power, and spreading himself like a green bay tree. Yet he passed away, and lo, he was not: yea, I sought him, but he could not be found. Mark the perfect man, and behold the upright: for the end of that man is peace." --Ps. 37:1, 2, 7, 9-11, 34-37.

We cannot control the inequalities of life; we must leave that to God. Heaven will be unequal too. Some will enjoy all the rewards Heaven has to offer because of a life spent in night-and -day service for the Lord here. Others will be in Heaven "so as by fire" without any fruit and therefore without any rewards. Are we work- ing so hard here for equal pleasures, equal wealth or equal position with the worldly crowd that we have forgotten to work for the riches of Heaven? Well, never mind if life is not equal; Heaven is forever!

Just One Phrase

This probably indicates the small retaining capacity of my mind, but I'm going to admit something to you. It is a very rare thing if I can ever remember the entire general outline of a sermon. What usually happens is that the preacher, in the course of his message, uses one phrase or thought which strikes home and I get so thrilled or blessed or convicted by that one thought that I completely lose the rest of the sermon. The same is true of articles and books and songs which I read or hear. Nearly always, when I have been greatly blessed, it is by the simplest, least profound thought in the whole message or song.

Sometimes the phrase which stands out in my mind has no special significance to other people, but that does not keep it from meaning a great deal to me. For instance the week of my wedding I found myself singing over and over again one single phrase from the WEDDING HYMN by Wendell Loveless:

"Joy comes at last, crowning all the days of longing . . ."

It seemed that I had loved Don for so long (three years to be exact) and now finally the wedding day was almost here! That one phrase seemed to be the sum of all my feelings.

One Sunday evening when I was especially troubled about something, I sat in church discouraged while the congregation around me sang the hymn, "All the Way My Saviour Leads Me." Suddenly one phrase came through to me which has since been a blessing time and time again in my life. It is the second line of the first verse:

"Can I doubt His tender mercy, Who through life has been my Guide?"

Now, in any time of perplexity, I find that my heart still races back to that sweet and haunting phrase which never fails to bring rest and comfort.

When I was still a very young girl I sat at a campfire service where many, many young people dedicated their lives to the Lord. To

143

this day I can't remember the title nor the theme of the message, nor even the text, but I do remember this simple thought:

"If you would live a successful Christian life, do not look behind you; you will become discouraged. Do not look around you; you will be disillusioned. Do not look in front of you; you will be afraid. Look up to Jesus; He will show you where to go."

This week in my daily Bible reading I have been going through the Psalms again. How rich that part of the Scripture always seems to be! I am always amazed at how many times one can read through the Book tracing only one thought at a time, and never, never exhaust the possibilities for blessing. In my reading this time the verse which has so completely captivated my heart and thoughts is Psalm 145:8:

"The Lord is gracious and full of compassion; slow to anger, and of great mercy."

I am not an especially patient person. I am nearly always frustrated with my own failings and shortcomings. Unfortunately, I often expect far too much of those around me as well.

And so you can see what a constant source of wonder it is to me that the Lord, righteous and perfect though He is, should be "slow to anger, and of great mercy." All week long that phrase has been singing and ringing in my heart. How marvelous! How amazing! Just one phrase . . . "slow to anger, and of great mercy"--but how full of meaning!

144

Hide-And-Seek

There are few sounds sweeter to a mother's ear than that of her children playing happily together in the way and place they are supposed to play! As far as I am concerned, the only thing which sounds more pleasant is to hear a Daddy's laughter mingled with the children's voices as they play.

Just the other night Daddy Don got home from work just a little earlier than usual and so he was playing a game of Hide-and-Seek with the children while I finished getting dinner ready. I was enjoying the giggles and squeals of delight when I suddenly remembered something I had wanted to tell my husband all day. It wasn't hard to find his hiding place. In the middle of the bedroom stood Baby Don gleefully pointing to his daddy's feet sticking out from behind the bed! I watched the game for a little while, deciding that my point of information could wait for a more opportune time. Carol, who was "seeking," was wandering around the living room looking behind curtains and chairs and

saying, "Where's Daddy? Where's Daddy?" so I thought I'd give her a little hint.

"Why don't you look in the back part of the house?" I said.

She gave me one of those looks reserved for people who don't know the rules of the game. "No, Mommy, don't you understand? I'm supposed to look EVERYWHERE ELSE first!" I smiled to myself and decided I'd better go back into the kitchen and finish my dinner. Of course Carol knew where to find her daddy--but it just wouldn't be a game if she went to find him too quickly!

Later, as I stood at the kitchen stove stirring gravy, I thought about the game of Hide-and-Seek we so often play with our Heavenly Father. He makes His presence so obvious in so many different ways--by His daily provision of food and shelter, by the good health which He gives, by the fellowship of loved ones and friends, and especially by the constant communication He offers us through His Word. And yet, somehow, we feel we must go through the ritual of "playing the game." We know that He has told us how and where to find Him in time of need, but we hesitate to go there directly. Instead, we

145

go through a formal routine of praying as though the piety of our words or the amount of repetition had anything at all to do with the nearness of God's ear or the tenderness of His loving heart.

We sometimes say, "Well, I must not ask God for this or that because the request does not fulfill all the biblical requirements for getting prayers answered." Occasionally someone says, "I know I can pray for what I need but I don't think it would be right to ask for something I merely want." I have even heard a mother say, "I'm afraid to ask for such-and-such; if I don't get an answer, my children will think God doesn't answer prayer."

All of these statements indicate that for many of us prayer is a game, a respected ritual which shows our spirituality but does nothing for our hungry, needy hearts. Perhaps the simple motto, "Pray Anyway" could revolutionize our prayer lives. Do you doubt that your request will fit God's requirements? Then pray anyway--the more you ask the easier it will be for Him to make the prayer fit the requirements! Do you hesitate to ask for some personal desire? Pray anyway--He loves to pro-

vide for the happiness of His children! Are you afraid you do not have enough faith to see your prayers answered? Pray anyway--the Lord is more concerned about His reputation as a Prayer-answering God than you are. He will see that your children learn that He is quick to hear.

Hide-and-Seek is a fine game for little children to play with their human daddies, but it will not do for us to play with our Heavenly Father. Hurry! He is patiently waiting. Go find Him at once!

"Ask, and it shall be given you; seek, and ye shall find; knock, and it shall be opened unto you: For every one that asketh receiveth; and he that seeketh findeth; and to him that knocketh it shall be opened."--Matt. 7:7, 8.

"If Only . . . "

Most of us spend at least some part of our lives reviewing things that are already past, and all too often our reflections include a regretful, "If only I had known how things would turn out!"

Once when our little daughter Carol was very small I had occasion to repeat to myself that futile "if only . . ." over and over again. I had allowed Carol to play on the basement steps while I was doing a washing, since she was already quite skilled at stair climbing. I reasoned that if she should happen to fall, I would be right below where I could either catch her or break her fall. However, in the process of opening the door to the kitchen at the top of the stairs, she lost her balance and fell, not down the steps, but underneath the guardrail, plunging headfirst to the cement floor below. I could not get to her in time, of course, and soon we were rushing her to the hospital where it was discovered that she suffered a fractured skull.

For weeks and weeks I tormented myself with foolish speculation as to how things might have been. "If only I had done my washing on Tuesday instead of Monday," I said. "If only I had kept my little girl off the stairs! If only I had watched her more closely, etc., etc., etc.!" All my self-criminations were useless because they were too late. The damage had been done. There is no way any of us can make the wheels of time go backward. I am happy to say that the Lord restored our little girl to full health without any aftereffects whatever, for which we were very grateful. Still, the anxiety and expense of such an experience are not soon forgotten.

Just last week a little 7-year-old girl in a nearby community was murdered by a 13-year-old boy. Any crime where the criminal and victim are both children seems unbelievably tragic, but this one seemed even more so because nearly everyone concerned with either the young murderer or the little girl had a poignant "if only . . ." to add to the sadness of the story. The boy's stepfather regretted that he had not spent more time with his son. The girl's father agonizingly rebuked himself for having sent a little child out to buy cigarettes after sundown. (Perhaps he even wished

147

he had never learned to smoke!) The pastor of the good evangelical church which the boy had attended said he felt the tragedy would not have occurred "if only . . ." the boy had kept coming to church. No doubt the Sunday School teacher who spent an hour with the boy in jail said to himself, "If only I had worked just a little harder to win him to Christ, etc." I can imagine that the boy's mother even now repeats to herself a thousand wishes that this or that had been done differently in the past thirteen years, as the boy was growing up.

I have often wondered how many times Adam said to himself, "If only I had listened to God instead of Satan . . ." or if perhaps David tortured himself with the thought of how differently his children might have turned out had he not given in to temptation during that one sleepless night. And what of Pilate who failed to heed the urgent warning of his wife, "Have nothing to do with this just man"? Saddest of all must be that bitter wail in Hell of the millions who cry, "IF ONLY I had listened to the pleading of my loved ones! IF ONLY I had turned from my sin! IF ONLY I had given my life to Christ while there was still time!"

All the regrets and tears we may shed about what might have been will not change history. The past is gone. But perhaps the Lord in His mercy will help us to take warning to do what we can do and ought to do while there is still time.

148

Change of Seasons

Hasn't it been a lovely fall? Here in the midwest the sugar maples have been especially colorful. I don't remember when the whole countryside ever looked more glorious in its autumn hues than it did this year. I wonder what makes the colors brighter some years than others? Perhaps it is the amount of rain throughout the summer or the timing of the first frost. Whatever the reasons, the results this fall have been so beautiful. Long after most of the summer flowers were gone, our climbing roses just kept on blooming, and our hardy mums didn't even begin to show themselves until after the frost. I saw some blooms even yesterday defying the first flurries of snow. They almost seem to enjoy the sharp wind and icy fall rains that ruin the other flowers.

There are so many nice things about the autumn. We have been enjoying new crisp yellow delicious apples at our house for weeks. Big, beautiful golden pumpkins have been advertised for only a dime apiece, so I must hurry to get some for pies. The canned pumpkin is certainly convenient, but there is something extra special about spicy pumpkin pie "made from scratch." And since our Daddy Don needs to put on a little weight, I will probably splurge a little and buy a half pint of whipping cream to make the pumpkin pie complete!

The fall weather brings about changes in our living habits, too. The children are not quite so early to rise since it stays dark so much later in the morning. That means the afternoon naps are shorter. The after-supper playtime now goes on in the house rather than outside which makes for more confusion and noise but also for more family "togetherness."

This is the time of year when all the sewing I have intended to do all year comes out of the boxes and drawers and some of it actually gets done! The old rocking chair which has badly needed recovering for more than a year is finally sporting new home-fashioned upholstery, and the flannel pajamas planned a year ago for the whole family are finally in the cutting-out stage.

Isn't it nice that the Lord provides changes for us--changes in weather, in interests, in occupation, in surroundings, in work to do? Routine work becomes so much more exhilarating after a break of some sort and even favorite pastimes are made more enjoyable when spaced between jobs involving some drudgery.

My sister, Mary Lloys Himes, has been flat on her back in bed for several weeks now--put there by doctors' orders. Since she has always been especially busy and active--raising four children, helping neighbors, teaching a Sunday School class, playing the piano and singing in the church choir, the drastic change from her usual busy life to one of almost complete inactivity has been hard. But when I was there visiting the other day she told me of some of the blessings this time has brought. She said she had never realized how kind friends and neighbors could be in helping the family, bringing in food, etc. (though I must add that she has done that sort of thing for many years). She said that the time one has for reading and meditation has been especially precious. And then she added, "I hadn't realized until now how much fun it was to make yeast bread. I can hardly wait to get my hands into some dough again!"

Changes do not always appear to be a blessing. Most of us would prefer that the sky be always blue, health always excellent, finances always in good order, friends always close by. But the Lord gives us changes--both good and bad--and the changes are always for our ultimate happiness. Summer was lovely; fall has been good, too. Winter is coming. And with its prospect of dark days, bitter wind and hampering snowstorms, let us thank God that He gives us changes--as in weather, so in life--to make our lives rich and full.

". . . I have learned, in whatsoever state I am, therewith to be content. I know both how to be abased, and I know how to abound: every where and in all things I am instructed both to be full and to be hungry, both to abound and to suffer need. I can do all things through Christ which strengtheneth me."--Phil. 4:11-13.

Thanksgiving

How will you spend Thanksgiving Day at your house?

Will there be friends and loved ones to share the bounties of your table? Will your home be filled with the smell of good food and with the sound of laughter and praise? Will there be gospel music coming from radio or phonograph (or better yet--from the throats of those gathered around your table)? Will you spend some time really and truly thanking the Lord for all His blessings--naming them one by one? I hope so.

Of course thanksgiving ought to be a day-by-day habit but I am glad a day is formally set aside each year for that purpose. Many will desecrate the day with drinking and reveling and feasting immoderately, and thousands more will eat their turkey and enjoy their friends without even a thought for the one who provides all the blessings of life. But it seems to me that is all the more reason for those of us who love the Lord to make it a time of joy and praise to God.

Sometimes Christians get the idea that anything happy or enjoyable must surely be unspiritual. But I'm certain the Lord delights in our joy and our feasting when we do it in His name, always remembering that the good things we possess are gifts from His bountiful hand. One of the earliest thanksgiving celebrations most surely had God's sanction. In the day of Queen Esther, after the Jews were wonderfully rescued from the hand of wicked Haman, Mordecai sent letters to all the Jews in the provinces of King Ahasuerus telling them:

". . . that they should keep the fourteenth day of the month Adar, and the fifteenth day of the same, yearly, As the days wherein the Jews rested from their enemies, and the month which was turned unto them from sorrow to joy, and from mourning into a good day: that they should make them days of feasting and joy, and of sending portions one to another, and gifts to the poor." --Esther 9:21, 22.

Perhaps your Thanksgiving Day will be a quiet one spent alone or on a hospital bed or with Sorrow as your nearest companion. Perchance the dinner you eat will be a meager one. Maybe the uncertainty of the future clouds the brightness of the day for you. Can the human heart be expected to be thankful even under such circumstances?

There is a wonderful old Swedish Thanksgiving hymn which answers the question so beautifully:

"Thanks to God for my Redeemer;
Thanks for all Thou dost provide!
Thanks for times now but a memory;
Thanks for Jesus by my side!
Thanks for pleasant, balmy springtime;
Thanks for dark and dreary fall!
Thanks for tears by now forgotten,
Thanks for peace within my soul!

"Thanks for prayers that Thou hast answered,
Thanks for what Thou dost deny!
Thanks for storms that I have weathered,
Thanks for all Thou dost supply!
Thanks for pain, and thanks for pleasure,
Thanks for comfort in despair!
Thanks for grace that none can measure,
Thanks for love beyond compare!

"Thanks for roses by the wayside,
Thanks for thorns their stems contain!
Thanks for home and thanks for fireside,
Thanks for hope, that sweet refrain!
Thanks for joy and thanks for sorrow,
Thanks for heav'nly peace with Thee!
Thanks for hope in the tomorrow,
Thanks through all eternity!"

Strange paradox, isn't it--that a Christian can be content, yes--even thankful, with problems and disappointments and sorrow?

I don't know how you will spend Thanksgiving Day. As I said, I hope it will be filled with laughter and love and feasting and good fellowship. But if not, your dearest Friend will still be there. Whether or not you eat your fill of turkey and dressing and pumpkin pie, you may still feast upon that One who satisfies the hungry soul. If there is no sound of laughter and fellowship throughout the rooms of your home, there still can be the music of Heaven ringing in your heart.

God bless you, friend, and may you have a WONDERFUL Thanksgiving!

Just a Simple "Thank You"

I know Thanksgiving Day is all over but I am still on the subject of gratitude. All week long Shakespeare's potent lines have been running through my mind: "Blow, thou winter wind! Thou'rt not so unkind as man's ingratitude."

This past Halloween we had about 80 boys and girls come to our door "Trick or Treating." There were little tiny goblins and witches whose mothers could dimly be seen hovering in the background. And there were big high school boys and girls who came without any extra costumes--only the big bags into which they were gathering goodies. Many of them were neighbor children--some were strangers. We gave out bubble gum and candy until there was no more and then started giving whatever treats we could find in the house. One thing startled me as I thought about it afterwards--in fact, I might even say it scared me. Out of the 80 or so children who came to our door there were only about six who thought to say "thank you" without any prompting! Some-

times when a child walked away without a word I would say as gently as I knew how, "Don't I get a thank you?" Our three-year-old Jimmy was not quite so tactful. When he handed out the candy he said very bluntly, "Say 'thank you!'"

Even taking into consideration the excitement of that particular occasion and the natural thoughtlessness of children, can it be that we are raising a generation of thankless, ungrateful children because we ourselves are thankless and ungrateful?

How pleasant it makes the day when someone remembers to say "thank you" for some favor --no matter how small. When I was in college I once got a postcard in the mail from a friend with the simple message, "Thank you for the smile of encouragement you gave me when we passed in the hall yesterday. It was just what I needed to change my day into a happy one." I was so impressed I put the card up on my dresser as a reminder to smile a little more often.

I have a brother-in-law who says to his very small children after each meal, "Now be sure to thank Mommy for the good breakfast (dinner, lunch, etc.)" I like to have my children around his children because I notice they are quick to pick up the same habit! A "thank you" for a simple meal or routine task can make all the difference in the world as to how much a mother enjoys her work.

Sometimes I think we neglect to be grateful just because we are preoccupied. We get so used to receiving certain benefits and services that we forget what a little gratitude would do for the one who provides the benefit or service. In such a case, our pre-occupation becomes a selfishness, an ingratitude. Perhaps we excuse ourselves on the basis that we have "paid" for the service and thereby have no obligation to render a simple "thank you." But what an empty life it would be if all our relationships to those around us were based entirely on the exchange of money for commodities or for services received. I doubt if any kind of labor--common, domestic, or professional--would be worth the effort if the only payment ever rendered were cold cash, without ever a word of praise or gratitude. We all need the response of other human beings to make work profitable and happy.

Who would be blessed by a word of thankfulness from you today? Your husband, perhaps, who gives of his love and time to make you happy? Does your pastor need a "thank you" for his faithfulness in preaching the Word? Are there friends and neighbors whose kindnesses you have begun to take for granted? Are your children learning from you the habit of being grateful?

You no doubt remember how grieved the dear Lord Jesus was when only one of the ten lepers whom He had healed thought to give thanks (Luke 17:12-19). Then how pleased He must be to find His own children with thankful, loving hearts! Let's remember to say "thank you!"

A Limited Vocabulary

At fifteen months old, our little Don is not much of a talker. He makes lots of sounds, of course, complete with inflections, question marks and exclamation points! He can chatter for hours in his own baby-lingo saying lots of "words" that are entirely for his own amusement. His recognizable English vocabulary, however, is so far limited to the barest essentials--Momma, Daddy, bye-bye, dog and gum! Just yesterday he pulled my face down to his and said very earnestly, "Num-num-num" and then was very pleased when I got the message that he was hungry and wanted something to eat!

Most of the time Donnie gets his needs fulfilled by taking my hand and leading me into one room or another. Once there, he points in the general direction of whatever it is he needs and wants, and I am expected to know what he means. Of course I am not always successful on the first guess, but since I am his mother (and the mother of two older children who went

through the same process at the same age) I can usually interpret his requests.

On the other hand, little Don does not always understand my vocabulary. If I talk about the weather, the Berlin crisis, or the people down the block--that is all beyond his comprehension. Still, that in no way hinders our communication when we fellowship together. He has no difficulty whatever understanding what I mean when I say "I love you" because he can see the meaning in my face and feel the meaning in the tenderness of my touch and he returns love for love with little grunts of affection and soft baby arms around my neck. He knows what actions on the part of his big brother and sister denote playtime and doesn't have to be told when a game is in process. He can hear the shouts of laughter and watch the skipping and running even though he might not understand all the words they use while they play. When he hears the welcome call "Daddy's home!" he knows to run to the front door in gleeful anticipation of being swept into Daddy's arms for a hug.

Last of all, Donnie knows exactly the meaning of the word "no"--especially when it is said with a finger sternly pointed in his direction. He also knows that the command "leave it alone," when ignored, will probably mean getting his little backside paddled! How wonderful it is that God gives the communication of love between parents and babies without the direct necessity for completely understanding each other's vocabulary.

My vocabulary, too, must seem very limited to my Heavenly Father. So often I do not know how to express my needs and my deepest heart's desires to Him. Because of my own human frailty, I can only point in a general direction to show Him what it is I want out of life--then I must leave it to Him to fill each day with its own measure of joy and sorrow, work and rest, success and failure. He knows and loves me better than any human mother could know or love a human baby, and because of this, He anticipates my needs even before a single faltering, lisping request is uttered. My weak, undeveloped human mind has no capacity for communicating with Him about the unsearchable mysteries of the universe, of life and death, and eternity. But I can understand His infinite love and mercy, which He daily expresses in

so many ways; I can enjoy the privilege of His gracious bounty; and I can feel the faithful hand of discipline which He must administer from time to time.
Romans 8:14-16 says:

"For as many as are led by the Spirit of God, they are the sons of God. For ye have not received the spirit of bondage again to fear; but ye have received the Spirit of adoption, whereby we cry, Abba, Father. The Spirit itself beareth witness with our spirit, that we are the children of God."

W. E. Vine tells us that "ABBA is the word formed by the lips of infants, and betokens unreasoning trust; FATHER expresses an intelligent apprehension of the relationship. The two together expresses the love and intelligent confidence of the child."

Well, then--a limited vocabulary is not so bad when one is a member of the family of God!

Getting Ready for Christmas

Just imagine--Christmas is almost here! Somehow the months and weeks and days since we put away last year's wrappings and burned last year's tree have flown by and now it is time to start thinking about Christmas again. The merchants in our town hardly gave us time to enjoy the Thanksgiving holidays before they started hanging their tinsel and displaying an even more awesome array of Christmas merchandise than they did last year. Even with the threats of war abroad and economic unrest at home, Christmas buying will, in all probability, reach an all-time high.

In the middle of this type of situation, how does a Christian go about preparing for Christmas? A few take the position that since pagans have more or less taken over the holiday, those who know the Lord ought to ignore the day altogether. They miss the joy of the carols, the pleasure of giving and receiving, the special blessing of remembering again that the Saviour came to the earth as a tiny babe, born of a human mother.

On the other hand, so many of us get so caught up in the trappings of "getting ready" for Christmas that we, too, miss the blessing of what a Christmas celebration ought to be. We put ourselves into debt trying to outdo last year's gifts, and we work ourselves into a fever with so much extra shopping and partying and miscellaneous holiday activity. That leaves us little time for the sweet meditation and singing and reading that ought to be a big part of enjoying Christmas.

I've been thinking about what I ought to do to get ready for Christmas in the proper way and I've come up with a few suggestions that might be helpful to you too:

1. Let's start now having the whole family memorize the Christmas story from the Bible. If your family has already committed to memory the more familiar account from Luke 2, then have them work on the passages in Matthew (chapter 1, vss. 18-25 and chapter 2). Then you will be ready by Christmas Eve to have the whole family recite the story together --a most thrilling experience! You will be surprised at how fast the very tiny children will learn.

2. Encourage your children to start making some simple gifts for others. Besides the joy these will bring to those who receive the presents, your children will discover the special delight of giving of ones own self and labor.

3. Start now writing Christmas LETTERS to people who will perhaps be lonely during the holidays. It is always nice to receive a lovely, expensive card at Christmas, but nothing so warms the heart as a personal note reminding a distant missionary or loved one that he is remembered and prayed for. So often the special attention of a few written words will mean more to someone who is lonely than a more costly gift.

4. Plan to entertain some in your home to whom you can be a real blessing--preferably someone who will not be in a position to return your invitation. This might include some who will be far away from their own loved ones; some who because of poverty or other circumstances will not have much of a Christmas celebration; and perhaps some who have never experienced the joy of a really "Christian Christmas" because they have never met the Christ of Christmas. Most people feel sociable and open-hearted at Christmastime. That makes it a wonderful time to work at winning the lost!

5. Plan your giving to have some real spiritual impact. Millions of dollars are spent every year on gadgets, clothes and toys. That is fine, up to a point. There will no doubt be gadgets and clothes and toys under our tree too. But we need to remember that gadgets often prove to be impractical; clothes wear out, and toys soon lose their interest or are broken. Some portion of our Christmas money ought to be spent for life-changing books, good Christian records, (yes, and even a subscription to THE SWORD OF THE LORD!) The milkman, the paper boy, the garbage man--all are more likely to accept a small gift-wrapped booklet showing the way of salvation at this time of year than at any other. Take advantage of the open doors of Christmastime.

Let's make this a really Christian Christmas!

Unfinished Business

I am a great one for starting things. I'll bet I have enough projects started or planned to keep me busy for the next ten years!

For instance, there are some oil portraits of my children I started painting two years ago and have ALMOST finished. There is a water color still life which only needs a little background work and then it will be done. In my desk are three chapters of a book I started to write, plus the outline and ideas for several more. I have a wonderful collection of tested and proved recipes in my kitchen but they will probably never do anyone else any good because they are in such disorder. Some are merely clipped or torn from magazines; some have been hastily recorded on the backs of envelopes; some are so soiled as to be nearly unreadable, and all of them are thrown together in an old cookbook which is so shabby it has to be held together with a rubber band. Several times I have started to learn Franz Liszt's beautiful LIEBESTRAUM on the piano but I never work on it quite long enough to be able to play it through without stumbling here or there. And then there are the sewing projects which never quite get finished. What a pity to have never-used dress patterns (size 3) which were bought for my littlegirl nowgoing on five!

These are little personal projects, of course, which mainly influence only myself and my family and if that were as far as my "unfinished business" went perhaps it would not be too serious. But there have been jobs I promised the Lord I would do, too--jobs which were never completed.

There have been people I intended to visit and invite to church, but when they were not at home the first time I called, I somehow never got back for a second visit. New Christians who needed the encouragement and friendship I could have given somehow got neglected after my first or second attempt to be friendly. There have been matters about which I prayed earnestly--for awhile--but when the answer was slow in coming, I neglected to keep on praying. I wonder how many things would be different now, if I had just finished the job?

159

And why is it that so many important things in life get left half done?

Perhaps the biggest obstacle that blocks our progress is that we have the wrong incentive, or REASON FOR DOING. We secretly hunger for the praise or public acclamation that we might receive for doing the job. If that reward isn't quickly forthcoming, then somehow the task doesn't quite seem worth the effort of finishing. It rarely occurs to us to do a thing because it is RIGHT to do--whether anyone else knows about it or not.

Another reason we so often leave work unfinished is that we are just plain lazy. In the bright enthusiasm we feel at beginning something new, we forget to count the cost of what may be involved. The sacrifice holds a certain glory as long as it is in the distant future. I know a man, a graduate of one of America's outstanding Bible schools, who joyfully started out to preach but he soon discovered that a minister's wages are often small, the work difficult, and congregations often critical. It wasn't long before he gave up the ministry altogether and went into something which required less sacrifice.

Perhaps a third reason we leave so many jobs undone is that we are so easily distracted, so readily sidetracked. We are like horses needing blinders. We are lured away from what we are doing by everything going on around us-- the glamour of someone else's job, the discouragements of our own, the appeal of something new and different.

Wouldn't it be a wonderful thing if we could say, like Paul:

"I have fought a good fight, I have finished my course, I have kept the faith: Henceforth there is laid up for me a crown of righteousness, which the Lord, the righteous judge, shall give me at that day: and not to me only, but unto all them also that love his appearing."
--II Timothy 4:7, 8?

Let's finish the job!

Home for the Holidays

Are you finding this Christmastime to be the joyful, happy season you had hoped it would be? We've been singing the carols since the middle of November and I still haven't gotten my fill of them yet. Our little ones learned "There's a Song in the Air" for the first time this year and it has been very sweet to hear their voices singing it around the house.

I hope you are enjoying having the school children home for the holidays, though it no doubt means the house gets a little dirtier a little faster and there is always more work with cooking when everyone is home. Why don't you just let some of the regular work go and spend a little more time on family projects and games? By now it is too late for mailing Christmas cards; the gift wrapping and church Christmas programs are over and done with. This would be a wonderful time to do the special informal things with your own family--the sort of things children remember for years and years to come.

At our house popcorn-making--no matter how many times we've done it--is still a special treat. Daddy Don usually does the popping because he has become the family authority on just how it should be done. The oil must be at just exactly the right temperature so that all the kernels will pop, and the measurements of oil and corn must be exact. If there are more than a dozen unpopped grains in the bottom of the pan, then we all tease our "chief popper" about losing his touch! When we have a huge bowl filled, we all stuff ourselves far past the point of moderation!

This is a nice time for the family to spend some hours reading good books aloud together. I still remember how moved I was as a child when we read together the biography of John and Betty Stam--martyred missionaries to China. Of course family reading need not necessarily be limited completely to good Christian books. There are many classical children's books and even some "fun" books that are worth reading and which will add joy to family holidays. One of the most delightful books for reading aloud at Christmastime is THE BIRD'S CHRISTMAS CAROL by Kate Doug-

161

las Wiggin. It is not too long and contains a fair combination of laughs and tears for the whole family besides some spiritual truths worth pondering.

One of the things we have been enjoying most during the holidays is our record player-- now sporting a nice new needle. Somehow the same old records we play year after year sound new and bright with the improvement in sound the new needle brings. A friend has loaned us a recording of the fairy tale opera HANSEL AND GRETEL by Humperdinck (sung in English) and we are enjoying it immensely along with our own album of Handel's MESSIAH (a priceless possession!) and Fred Waring's CHRISTMAS TIME album, which contains many of the old favorite carols plus some less familiar ones as well.

However you spend the holiday hours when the children are home from school, I do hope you will make the dear Lord Jesus the source of all your joy and pleasure. And may His presence go before you right into the new year! God bless you every one!

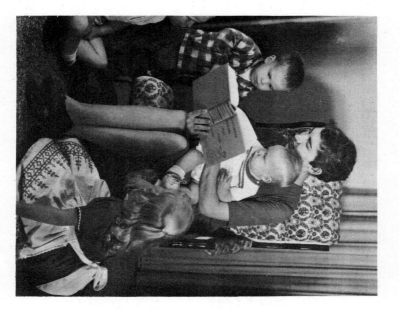

How He Guides

A happy and blessed New Year to you!

How will you celebrate the coming of 1962? No matter how gaily or carelessly other people may celebrate the arrival of a brand new year, I find the occasion a rather sobering one. A new year holds so many prospects--for good or for evil, for joy or for sorrow, for success or for failure. What folly it would be, to think of looking forward to the months ahead without spending some time seeking God's special guidance and leading. I think the Lord must surely give us new beginnings, new opportunities to start over, so that we will be encouraged to put the past with its failures and disappointments behind us and begin to serve Him in new dedication and blessing.

Did you ever stop to think how many different means the Lord uses to guide us and direct our pathway? Psalm 32:8 says, "I will instruct thee and teach thee in the way which thou shalt go: I will guide thee with mine eye."

I remember one time observing a message being given across a crowded room from a husband to a wife without a word ever being spoken! It was all done with the eyes. The wordless communique from the husband evidently said, "Your slip is showing" because the wife made a hasty and discreet adjustment to her skirt and the husband smiled to indicate that the message had been correctly received.

It goes without saying that to be led by the eye of God, we must be looking toward Him. Furthermore, to be guided by one's eye requires that the two parties involved must have a certain kinship of mind and purpose. We learn to see "eye to eye" with the Lord as we study His Word and then determine to obey it, regardless of the cost. A careless, blind Christian, absorbed in watching what the world is doing, will never experience the thrill of this special kind of guidance.

Sometimes the Lord guides us with His voice. Isaiah 30:21 says, "And thine ears shall hear a word behind thee, saying, This is the way, walk ye in it, when ye turn to the right hand, and when ye turn to the left."

Psalm 73:22-24 says, "So foolish was I, and

163

ignorant: I was as a beast before thee; Nevertheless I am continually with thee: Thou hast holden me by my right hand. Thou shalt guide me with thy counsel, and afterward receive me to glory." This is the kind of guidance we give to a little child when we hold him firmly by the hand. If you have ever walked down a busy street with very small children you know how many perils there are for little ones without the firm grasp of a parent's hand to guide them. They are so likely to dash suddenly in front of a car, to pet a strange dog or to put some forbidden object from the sidewalk into the mouth, or to wander off and be lost. A small child needs the hand of a careful mother or father. Sometimes we, too, as inexperienced children, need the firm hand of our Heavenly Father to guide us. When we have the Lord to hold us by the hand, we may stumble but we cannot fall; we may be tempted to turn aside toward some dangerous diversion, but we are restrained by His loving hand.

How good the Lord is to offer us His loving guidance for the coming year! For those who will keep their eyes on Him, He guides with His eye. He calls with His voice. For the inexperienced, He leads with His hand. Will you let Him guide you in the new year?

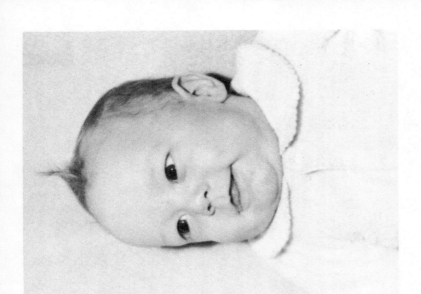

"The Best Laid Plans . . ."

Isn't it a satisfying experience to make plans and then have everything turn out just exactly as you hoped they would? When I know I am going to have an especially busy day, I usually make a list in the morning of the things I plan to get done throughout the day and then check each item off as it is finished. Unfortunately, I can't remember a single time in the past five years when I actually did accomplish absolutely everything I planned to get done in any one day. There are always so many unexpected interruptions--one would think I would eventually learn to put in the schedule a space for "Emergency Number One," "Interruption Number Two," etc.

We have a new baby at our house and I have been made aware again of how little one can do in arranging the events surrounding the birth of a baby. Since we already had a girl and two boys, everyone said that of course this one just MUST be a girl to even up the family. (Some might even have said it was poor planning to be having another baby when our youngest was only 15 months old.) Though I had no special concern about whether it would be a girl or boy, I WAS enjoying the fact that it was to arrive before Thanksgiving so that I would have plenty of time to get ready for the busy Christmas season. Besides, one of my good friends and neighbors was expecting a baby at the same time and we were looking forward to being in the hospital together.

As you may have already guessed, nothing went "according to schedule." Little Mark (our third boy!) arrived two weeks late, in the hustle and bustle of pre-Christmas preparation. All the extra cleaning and ironing and baking I had done three weeks earlier now needed to be done again. The laundry basket was full and the refrigerator was empty! By the time our new little boy and I were ready to come home from the hospital the three older children were fighting bad colds (complete with sore throats and earaches) and wouldn't you know--the baby and I then caught colds too! Another case of bad timing.

Now that little Mark is here and the children all well and the household fitting into some sort

of routine, there is no question but that everything turned out just right. Our baby boy is exactly what we have always wanted and somehow, in retrospect, we wonder how it mattered WHEN he arrived--especially since he seems to us so beautiful and healthy and so infinitely sweet.

God's sense of timing works so much better than ours. He plans events by their eternal consequence. Our temptation is to make plans according to the conveniences of the moment. Sometimes, when all the smoke has cleared away and we are left standing in the ashes of our best-laid plans, the Lord gives us a peek at His plans and tells us His reason for making ours void. But often we are required to wait until that moment when all the mysteries of Heaven will be open to our view. Until then, how sweet it is to lean heavily upon the blessed promise of God:

"Trust in the Lord with all thine heart; and lean not unto thine own understanding. In all thy ways acknowledge him, and he shall direct thy paths."--Prov. 3:5,6.

A Birthday Child

Do you remember the special delight of being a "birthday child" when you were very small?

As I was growing up, birthdays were made to be very important at our house even though money was scarce and gifts were often home-made. Mother always baked a certain kind of yellow cake for birthdays, and to this day whenever I taste a similar type of cake something inside me automatically says "Happy birthday!" Sometimes there was a new dress or new clothes for my doll--all made by a patient and loving mother. One year Daddy rigged up a pair of ingenious stilts made of large fruit cans and heavy wire. They were not dangerously high and they made such a wonderful "clop-clop" sound when I walked on them.

The birthday celebration usually began the Sunday before, when we would take extra pennies to Sunday School to put in the birthday bank--a penny for each year of age. I was painfully shy as a little girl so it was usually hard for me to go to the front of the room and drop in my pennies while the other children counted and then sang the birthday song. Still, there was something exciting about the extra attention and I always knew that when Sunday School was over dear old Mr. Crawford would give me a "birthday nickel" to spend for any-thing I wanted.

When the "real" birthday arrived, the day was special from beginning to end. There was an extra sweetness in being waked up with a birthday kiss and being prayed for in a special way at family devotions. Sometimes there was a birthday party with a few neighborhood chil-dren in the afternoon. Later in the day, usually at the supper table, there were more family rituals--a cake with candles, a gift or two, the singing of "Happy Birthday" and then a playful birthday spanking. How wonderful it was to have a birthday at our house! No matter how many children there were or how busy every-one was, there was always one day in the year which was our very own. There was no crisis too great or business too important to keep us from feeling especially loved and wanted on that day.

The most important event of my life took place the day I celebrated my fifth birthday. My memory is very clear of all that happened that day though it took place more than a quarter of a century ago. Breakfast was over and the older children had gone to school. My mother talked to me about what a big girl I was getting to be and how nice it was that I was now five years old. Then she asked me if I wouldn't like to let Jesus come into my heart and take away my sin. I had already been deeply conscious of my need of a Saviour and so I was happy and relieved to get the matter settled. Somehow it seemed especially wonderful that I was celebrating two birthdays all at the same time. After Mother and I had prayed together I asked if I could go down to Daddy's office at the church to tell him what I had done. Of course he was pleased and then he prayed with me too before I hurried on to tell others about my "two birthdays." (I might add here, that all five of my sisters were also led to the Lord by our parents in the home before they were six years old.)

Many birthdays have gone by since that all-important one when I became five years old, and they have all been happy ones--even with the new gray hairs of recent years, the extra tiredness and added cares of a growing family. Now my prayer and concern is that my own children will experience the joys of being able to celebrate both kinds of birthdays--the physical and the spiritual.

Most of us can do so much more for our children in a material way than our parents were able to do for us. Our birthday parties are complete with fancy hats and balloons and ice cream and expensive gifts. What a tragedy it would be if we gave our children the sweet heritage of happy birthday memories and yet neglected to teach them about the new birth. Birthdays are happy days--at least they ought to be --but their significance can only last a lifetime. A spiritual birthday can be celebrated throughout eternity. Let's make certain our children experience the joy of both kinds!

The Gift of Love

Christmas is over and done with. The decorations have been packed away for another year. The cards have been lovingly viewed and reviewed and then put away. The shedding pine tree has been burned. Thank-you notes have been written and mailed (at least I hope mine will be in the mail by the time you read this)! Without the clutter of dropping tinsel, Christmas boxes and leftover wrapping paper, the house has an empty, almost too-clean look about it. We are back to our workaday world of making a living, keeping house, going to church, caring for children--fulfilling obligations to society.

I hope I won't be misunderstood if I say that this year the sweetest part of Christmas turned out to be some of the things I received. The gifts of friends and loved ones are always precious--not because of their material value but because of the love and thoughtfulness they express. As far as I am concerned, one of the nicest gifts is a simple Christmas card which contains a personal note or expression of love, and we received so many of those this year.

My father has, for several years, given each of his six daughters a lovely dress at Christmastime. He has always done the shopping himself, choosing each dress to fit the taste and personality of each girl. This year he suffered an attack of flu just before Christmas and so there were no dresses under the tree. Instead there were small white envelopes addressed to each girl with money enclosed so that we could buy our own dresses. Along with the money I found a note in my envelope which said:

Dear Jessie:
    Happy Christmas! God bless you! A dress to remember me by--?

                                    Love, Dad

. . . and then there was a poem written in my father's hand:

**I hadn't a thing to give
And my heart was burning so!**

169

That love must speak and must caress
It could not speechless go.

So I gave myself instead
Of the gifts of gem or gold
My love, my joy, my hopes, my tears
I gave from my very soul.

As I hugged Dad's neck and thanked him, I asked who had written the lovely poem. It sounded to me like something Browning would have written. Daddy answered simply, "I wrote it for you." Right in the middle of all the excitement and laughter and noise of a family Christmas tree I had to go off in a corner and cry just a little--I was so moved at so tender an expression of a father's love. I couldn't have cared less whether there was money or a dress or anything else at all. The poem and the meaning of the poem meant more to me than anything else Dad could have given.

No doubt the Lord feels the same way about our giving. It is right to give of our money and time and attention to the Lord Jesus but the gift that surely brings Him the greatest joy is the gift of ourselves and our love.

In II Corinthians 8, the Apostle Paul gives a touching commendation of the church at Macedonia which gave liberally in "the abundance of their joy and their deep poverty." He says that they prayed ". . . with much intreaty that we would receive the gift, and take upon us the fellowship of the ministering to the saints. And this they did, not as we hoped, but first gave THEIR OWN SELVES to the Lord, and unto us by the will of God."

How precious is the gift of love!

Let's Be Sentimental!

In our practical, busy, modern world the word "sentimental" has a rather poor connotation. When we use the word to describe an individual, the meaning we intend is usually unfavorable. We mean that the person is overly-emotional -- going by feeling rather than logic.

I confess to being sentimental in every sense of the word. I can get weepy-eyed at the slightest provocation. I cry at weddings, when I see a parade, and always when I hear "The Star Spangled Banner." Lovely poetry, romantic books and beautiful music all move me to tears. When our little Mark Ray arrived just a couple of months ago, I was so thrilled at the wonder of actually watching his birth and hearing his first cry that I laughed and cried all at the same time. The nurses teased me about getting so sentimental about the birth of my fourth child. "That," they laughingly informed me "was to be expected of a mother having her firstborn--not her fourth!"

I can get sentimental and nostalgic when I see the first crocus of spring and when I smell the first bonfire of autumn. I get goosebumps everytime a brand new engagement ring. Reading the old love letters sent me by my husband during courting days still makes my heart do flip-flops. I sometimes weep when I read of the death of someone I didn't even know, and seeing a crippled child always brings a lump in my throat. Call me mawkish if you like; I admit to being incurably sentimental.

Webster's Dictionary says that "sentiment" is, among other things, "tender susceptibility." I rather like that definition. Is it so bad, really, to be so aware of the joys and sorrows, the mountains and valleys of life, that one is moved to some demonstration of feeling?

When I was very young I once wrote my Dad to say that I wished I did not always have to feel things so deeply. His answer was very sweet and very helpful and I still refer to it when I feel too deeply affected by the ups and downs of my own affairs or the affairs of others. The letter said, in part:

171

" . . . God gives to some an ardent nature. He gives some people great capacity for love and for loyalty. He gives some people dreams and other worldly-aspirations which the common run of people do not have. That makes for more suffering, but it makes also for more poetry in living and a wider scope of friends, and more joy in life. It is not a bad thing, but a good thing . . . ."

I feel certain that Jesus was sentimental in the sense that He was "tenderly susceptible" to the joys and sorrows of those around Him. Moved by the tears of those He loved, Jesus wept at the grave of Lazarus even though He knew Lazarus would shortly rise again. How touching was His grief over the troubles of Jerusalem which had already rejected Him as Messiah:

"O Jerusalem, Jerusalem, which killest the prophets, and stonest them that are sent unto thee: how often would I have gathered thy children together, as a hen doth gather her brood under her wings, and ye would not!"--Luke 13:34.

Luke 19:41 says, "And when he was come near, he beheld the city, and wept over it." Jesus was always aware of the burdens and needs of others; He was compassionate.

If being sentimental means that we feel the joys and the sadnesses of those around us; if being sentimental means that we are tenderly susceptible to the feelings of others--then let's be sentimental!

"Rejoice with them that do rejoice, and weep with them that weep. Be of the same mind one toward another."--Rom. 12:15, 16a.

Winter Blues

I've always been a great booster of midwestern weather, but after this week's deep-freeze temperatures, I'm ready to turn in my loyalty badge and move to Florida!

When it gets way down to 20 below (as it did this morning), everything seems to go wrong. In the first place, the car won't start. When it does finally go, we creep at a snail's pace, hoping we don't slide into a snowbank or ditch as so many cars around us are doing. We fuss because the snowplows are so slow in cleaning the streets, and when they do come, we fuss because they pile up the snow in front of our just-shoveled driveway.

At home things are just as bad. The furnace runs every minute, and still we complain that the air seems chilly. The doors freeze shut; even the brine in the water softener freezes. Our new expensive storm windows still do not keep the little ridge of ice from forming on our window sills. We stumble through knee-high drifts to take out our garbage and burn our papers. The milk bottles at the back door break with cold. The children chaff at having to be inside. They quarrel a little more than usual, and there seems to be more bumps and tumbles and tears and broken things. I feel edgy because the children are underfoot and I worry a little because I know my husband is likely to have a little trouble with the car coming home from work. Somehow I feel uncomfortably confined to my usually pleasant home, isolated from friends and stores and church by the great white waves of glistening snow outside. Patience wears thin. The whole town seems irritable and short-tempered with the little problems of getting around through the ice and snow to run our errands and visit our friends and go to business.

Somehow our winter problems manage to follow us to church. The attendance drops with the thermometer and even the most faithful and conscientious teachers straggle in late, delayed by sluggish cars. The church bus won't run and so willing workers hustle all over town picking up children who otherwise could not come. The halls are filled with wet boots and overcoats and confusion. Department secretaries try frantically to come up with accurate records of attendance as the late-comers trickle in. By the time the morning service begins, everyone is so exhausted and harassed that they completely miss the blessing of the first song. With that kind of beginning, it takes a mighty warm pastor to break through the ice and get to the hearts of the people.

Everybody is saying, "Won't it be nice when the cold wave is ended?"

Meanwhile, our God remains the same in fair weather and foul. He who slept through the storm on the Sea of Galilee still controls the elements and uses each circumstance of life to His own glory. His purposes are not frustrated by ice and snow or by rain or by heat. His mercies are as faithful in winter as they are in summer, springtime and harvest.

Then don't let the cold get you down. Just enjoy the sunshine of God's love.

About My Children

Just recently several have written, asking that I tell a little bit about my children. Now that is a subject upon which I can really wax eloquent! I might add that it is also a subject upon which I am entirely prejudiced and biased! Like all mothers, I love to talk about my children.

Carol Joy, our oldest child and only girl, has just reached the exciting age of five years. I am happy to say that she has inherited the blond hair, fair complexion and blue eyes of her daddy. (She is very proud of this resemblance and so am I!) Carol loves music of every sort and is quick to catch the tune of any song which pleases her. If she can't remember the words, she simply fills in with words of her own choice and the results are often hilarious. Carol is extremely sensitive and tender-hearted. Her early awareness of her own sin made it easy for us to win her to the Lord just before her fourth birthday. She is fascinated with motherhood--longs for the day when she will

175

175

have a real live baby of her own. That makes her a real help in the care of Baby Mark.

Jimmie, at three-plus, is brown-eyed, blond, solid as a meatball and (to use the phrase all parents love; is "all boy." In disposition he is placid and matter-of-fact. Jimmie is extremely fond of machinery of all types--can keep happy for hours hitching and unhitching toy trucks and trains. If he is deeply absorbed in anything he is likely to walk into a blank wall or stumble over a piece of paper. Although he appears shy, Jimmie loves company and warms up easily to a friendly voice.

Donnie, 17 months old, is a livewire. From morning until night he is constantly investigating--opening drawers and cabinets, climbing onto tables and dressers and trying everything his big brother and sister do. He already loves to tease and can sometimes make life uncomfortable for his big brother and sister. His unusual energy and strong will mean that he often requires more spankings. His happy smile and impish ways make him a favorite of babysitters and friends.

Baby Mark is only seven weeks old and so he has the advantage of appearing almost perfect

in his mother's eyes. He is a pleasant, happy baby who cries only rarely and will smile and "talk" when spoken to. He seems not to mind the constant petting and loving he gets from all the little ones at our house. What a joy he is to us all!

Isn't it an interesting quirk of nature that although we as parents have a chance to know more of the failings and weaknesses of our own children, we are at the same time the most prejudiced in their favor! While teachers and friends and acquaintances may love our children only when they are good, we love them all the time--good or bad. That is one of the blessings they experience because they belong to us. When they do wrong we are sad, and perhaps we punish them, but we keep on loving them just the same.

I am often reminded in my relationship with my children, of the Lord's tender compassion toward us. Our Heavenly Father is certainly more aware of the failings of His children than any earthly father could be and yet He keeps on loving the frailest and poorest Christian. When Satan, the great accuser, comes before our Father to remind Him of our sins, He remembers instead that we are His dearly beloved children whose sins are covered and forgiven. How sweet it is to realize that our God is pre-judiced toward His own children.

"Like as a father pitieth his children, so the Lord pitieth them that fear him."--Ps. 103:13.

The Single Girl

Not too long ago a friend wrote and asked "Why do you say the 'Kitchen Window' column is for wives and mothers. I'm neither a wife nor a mother and I read it all the time." Frank-ly, I was pleased and flattered and decided that perhaps she does have a point. Though every woman lives her own life in different circum-stances and different situations, we all share the need for fellowship and the common goal of wanting our lives to be full and fruitful. And so, wives and mothers, you listen while I say a good word for the single girl!

I have a special fondness for single women. Two of my favorite people are the girls who come to stay with my children when I have to be away from home. They work all day in the Sword of the Lord office and still manage to be patient and cheerful when they come to our house in the evening. They have the remarkable gift of be-ing able to combine objectivity with love (some-thing which is hard for mothers to achieve.) It is a standard joke at our house that if little

Donnie has been difficult all day he will be as sweet as pie for Mary Ann. And how he loves her! Of course I am fond of the girls because they are good to my children but there is a kinship of spirit that goes beyond children or marriage or singleness. We like to have them around for their own selves.

So much of my life and ambitions have been shaped by the influence of women who put their calling above a home. I remember especially several Christian schoolteachers who gave dedicated service at great personal sacrifice. My model of efficiency has always been dear Miss V. (Viola Walden, my father's secretary) who manages to turn out mountains of work day in and day out and still finds time to remember everybody's birthday and other special days. Miss Fairy (Fairy Shappard, head of THE SWORD advertising department) was my chief confidante in high school and college days. Somehow my schoolday triumphs were more exciting when shared with her and my disappointments never quite so bad with the gentle sympathy and advice she gave. Miss Fairy, though having no children of her own, has been a "mother" to many.

Miss Fairy Shappard　　**Miss Viola Walden**

I'm a great matchmaker. I get lots of fun out of introducing people who seem well suited to each other, and it is especially exciting if they do actually decide they love each other and then eventually marry. But I am becoming more and more aware of the fact that the wedding ring is no longer the symbol of complete happiness and fulfillment. Don and I, in our work with youth in churches and camps, have found that girls who marry extremely young, who marry without the positive assurance of God's blessing, or who marry because they fear the social stigma of being single, are nearly always courting disaster.

In my premarital days I formed some wonderful friendships with other girls who were working--not dull, unhappy, bored girls, but young women who were doing exactly what they wanted to do, working joyfully for the Lord. In the years since some have married; some have not. Some are living lives of more complete fulfillment and service for the Lord because they are married; others have found that they chose God's second best in choosing marriage. The secret of happiness is always, whether we are married or single, finding and accepting God's perfect plan.

In I Corinthians 7, the Apostle Paul says that "the unmarried woman careth for the things of the Lord, that she may be holy both in body and in spirit. . ." Then he adds this word for all of us to remember:

". . . the time is short: it remaineth, that both they that have wives be as though they had none; And they that weep, as though they wept not; and they that rejoice, as though they rejoiced not; and they that buy, as though they possessed not; And they that use this world, as not abusing it: for the fashion of this world passeth away."--I Cor. 7:29-31.

What Do You Know About Heaven?

Last Friday afternoon, the Fairhaven Rest Home in Moline, Illinois, was a little quieter than usual. The nurses, so used to seeing old people die, were a little sad and tearful. Grandma Sandberg had peacefully slipped out of her frail, 92-year-old body and gone to be with her Lord. Dear Grandma, always joyful, always thankful, would never again cheer the hearts of the patients and staff with her smile and her song.

We had told our children that their daddy's grandmother was very sick and might not live long, and we explained how much happier she would be in Heaven where she would never again be tired or sick or old.

Three-year-old Jimmie listened carefully and then asked, "Is it her leg?" (He remembered that Grandma had fallen last spring and broken her hip.) "If that's what is wrong with her, maybe we could fix it with Scotch tape." How does one explain to a practical-minded little

boy that not everything in life can be fixed with a bit of glue or a strip of tape? Carol was concerned about how Grandma would get to Heaven. "Would she fly like a bird? Would the angels come and carry her there?" Jimmie wanted to know if she WANTED to be with Jesus. The questions were not meant to be foolish. They only seemed so to our adult minds because we are used to passing over and ignoring anything we don't understand.

Later I got to thinking how strange it is that the most important questions of life and death are left to chance by millions and millions of people. If you should ask them, "Where will you spend eternity?" they will answer glibly, "I don't think we can know such things until after death," or they will say they "hope" to be in Heaven. No searching for certainty, no determination to find out. People who wouldn't think of letting a strange sound in a car go uninvestigated, or a physical illness go untreated, go about their business day by day ignoring the warning of their own conscience, "the wages of sin is death. . . ."

Grandma Sandberg knew where she was going, and she had the glad certainty that her fare had already been paid. During the last months of her life, while she was in the rest home she sang for anyone who would listen (usually in Swedish) and the theme of her song was often about Heaven. Her favorite was the old Swedish hymn, "Hans Skall Opne Parle Porten":

"He the pearly gates will open,
    So that I may enter in,
For He purchased my redemption
    And forgave me all my sin. . . ."

How happy Grandma's arrival at the pearly gates must have been--to be greeted by the mother and father she had kissed goodbye in Sweden so many years ago, by her two sons who had gone on before and best of all, to be welcomed by her Saviour.

Perhaps it is not too important after all, where we will spend our vacation, whether we ever get to see the other side of the world, or even whether our scientists will ever get to the moon. The question is--what do you know about Heaven? Will YOU spend eternity there?

"Let not your heart be troubled: ye believe in God, believe also in me. In my Father's house are many mansions: if it were not so, I would have told you. I go to prepare a place for you. And if I go to prepare a place for you, I will come again, and receive you unto myself; that where I am, there ye may be also. . . I am the way, the truth, and the life: no man cometh unto the Father, but by me."--John 14:1-3, 6.

Learning to Cope

Not too long ago the Women's Fellowship of our church had a meeting where we discussed the subject, "What Do You Do With Your Time?" Different women, representing several different home situations, told how they spent a typical day--how much of their time was used for the Lord, how much for housework, how much for leisure, etc. Among those participating were: the wife of an airline pilot who has no children but a difficult, irregular schedule to cope with; a single, working girl who spends at least three evenings a week in church work; a mother of five school-age boys who raises her family for the Lord without the help of a godly husband, and a pastor's wife who has a family of seven (ages 7-1) and manages to teach a Sunday School class, a weekday Bible class for women and writes a weekly crossword puzzle on the side!

By the time those women got through telling how they got their work done, I didn't know whether to be discouraged by my own inadequa-

cies or whether to be challenged to do better myself! In the discussion which followed, one mother was asked how she managed to get everything done she had to do. The answer was simple. She said, "I just learned to face the fact that I could do anything I ought to do."

Since then I've been thinking over that simple statement to see what effect it might possibly have on my life if I would let it. These were my conclusions. You can take them for what they are worth:

1. First, I must ask the Lord's guidance in deciding what my "oughts" really are. Once my obligations are clear, then I have a right to ask and expect strength from the Lord to get them done.

2. Making up my mind that I WILL do what I OUGHT to do, whether I like it or not, should relieve the tension of inwardly fighting against my duty. Most of the time it is not the hard work that hurts us--only our rebellion at having to do it.

3. Perhaps this is merely another way of covering the second point but it is worth repeating: I will need to find joy in my work and pride in its accomplishment (even those little

chores which have to be done over and over again). Furthermore, I will have to remember that if it is right to do, then it's right to do cheerfully. Personally, I've found that singing while I work makes it a little more fun and often helps to speed my fingers and my feet in whatever I am doing.

4. If I am to make the best use of my working hours, then I must start with the rest of heart and mind provided by a time of prayer and reading God's Word. No working day will be as successful as it might have been if it is not begun with prayer. And any time I am feeling overburdened with too much to do or with too many problems, then I will need to seek the Lord again. How well the hymn by Mrs. M. A. Kidder sums it all up:

Ere you left your room this morning
Did you think to pray?
In the name of Christ, our Saviour,
Did you sue for loving favor,
As a shield today?

O how praying rests the weary!
Prayer will change the night to day!

So, when days seem dark and dreary,
Don't forget to pray.

What is it that really wears us out? Is it the 24-hour job of fixing meals and mending socks and washing dishes and taking care of children and pleasing our husbands and serving the Lord? Or can it be rather that we are exhausted with tension headaches and stomach ulcers and a thousand frustrations because we have not asked the Lord to give us the joy of learning to cope with all He gives us to do.

I Am a Modernist

I have a terrible confession to make. I am a modernist. (Don't stop reading here!)

Oh, you'd never know it at a casual glance. I read my Bible every day (almost). I thank God for the food every time I sit down to the table (at least I go through the form of thanking God). I go to Sunday School, two services on Sunday and midweek prayer meeting. (Of course I don't always contribute any warmth to the services but at least I'm there.) I can talk about spiritual things with a familiarity that borders on glibness and sometimes I even try to talk to lost people about being saved (hoping they bring up the subject first)!

. . .And yet I am a modernist. Isn't a modernist a person who refuses to take the Bible literally, or who accepts as truth only the parts he wishes to believe? Doesn't a modernist believe that Jesus Christ was only a man--good perhaps, but not the Holy, Omniscient, All-seeing Creator of the Universe, Son of the Living God?

The fact of the matter is, I am a fundamentalist too--from my chin up! My head knows that the Bible really is true from beginning to end and that God meant for me to believe every word whether I understand it or not. Furthermore, my head is convinced that the Lord loves me and has the power to do anything and everything for me.

Still, there is a part of me that makes the Word of God a book of fables and that makes my God a frail, inadequate Being who has neither the power nor interest to care about the course of my life.

The Bible says that there is a Hell which burns with everlasting fire for those who reject the Saviour--yet I go day after day without ever warning and pleading with those who are headed there. Something in my cold, backslidden heart evidently refuses to believe that Hell can be as terrible or as imminent as the Bible says it is. Does not that make me a modernist?

The Bible says, "If ye shall ask any thing in my name, I will do it" (John 14:14). My heart answers, "That couldn't possibly be true"; and so the only kind of prayer I indulge in is a ritualistic kind of exercise that begins at my lips

184

and goes about as high as the ceiling. No wonder I seldom see prayers answered. I don't REALLY believe the Bible means what it says. Am I not then a modernist?

The Bible says, "Trust in the Lord with all thine heart; and lean not unto thine own understanding. In all thy ways acknowledge him, and he shall direct thy paths" (Prov. 3:5, 6). But I say to myself, "No, that couldn't be entirely true. If I am to get anywhere, I'll have to do the planning and scheming myself. God can't really know what's good for me as well as I know myself! Therefore I fret and worry and plan and then when I get everything worked out as I like--perhaps I will let the Lord know what I intend to do.

Does all this sound silly? It IS silly, but worse than that it is terribly tragic. What foolish kind of reasoning is it that we will trust the Lord Jesus with our own soul's salvation and yet make His Word a lie by our cold, unbelieving hearts! We trust Him with the biggest thing--our own souls--yet somehow we feel we can't trust Him with every little single insignificant part of our lives.

Lord, forgive us for our modernistic hearts.

How Many Pounds of Dirt?

Do you get as tired of dirt as I do?

Everywhere I turn there is something dirty that needs to be made clean again. What a constant battle it is--dirty little overalls, dirty walls, dirty windows, dirty dishes, dirty hands, dirty shoes! I wonder how many pounds of dirt go through my house in a single week? No doubt the little throw rug that catches the mud and dirt at our front door contains several ounces all by itself and the vacuum sweeper collects an unending amount. I suppose there is no way to estimate how much is contained in an average house--much less an un-average one like ours! Even our sweet baby who never touches the floor or the ground outside gets dirt in his fat little creases and has to be washed just like everything else in the house!

Of course the problem doesn't belong exclusively to the housewife. I have seen the big skyscrapers in Chicago so filthy with soot and dust that the dirt had to be actually sand-blasted off. And what a job the street cleaners have in the spring trying to remove all the winter's accumulation of cinders and salt and miscella- neous debris from the city streets.

Automobiles, farm machinery, office equip- ment, factory machinery, household appliances --all need to be cleaned to function well. Dust particles in the air can cause allergies. Dirt in water can cause disease. Metals and cement and stone are worn down by the friction caused by dirt. There is no end to the grief dirt can cause. All in all, it would seem to be one of mankind's worst enemies.

On the other hand, did you ever stop to re- alize that dirt provides our source of life? The fruits and vegetables we eat must depend on earth for their existence. The animals which produce our meat in turn eat the vegetation that grows out of the earth. More wonderful yet, God reached down and took a handful of dirt to make the very first man, and each human body created since has been made of the very same stuff. Earth loans us her substance for the days of our years--whether few or many--and then claims her own possession when we die. Whether we like to admit it, we are all--rich

and poor, renowned and unknown, old and young, lovely and unlovely, brilliant and ignorant-- made of common earth. Rather a shocking fact, don't you think?

What a poignant statement is found in Genesis 3:23. After Adam and Eve had sinned the Bible says, "Therefore the Lord God sent him forth from the garden of Eden to till the ground FROM WHENCE HE WAS TAKEN." The magnificent creatures God had formed for His own fellow- ship and joy were to live by digging the very dirt from which they were made!

Dirt is not a very pleasant thing, is it? And the very fact that we ourselves are made of dust only reminds us that the earthly part of us is really of very little value.

Well, we CAN live with dirt. Indeed, God has made even the cursed ground to be a bless- ing to us day by day in the food it provides and in the work it requires of us. The very fact that we must struggle with it encourages our dependance upon our God.

The dirt which brings the greatest sorrow is that which collects in our hearts and soils what we say and what we do. Just as our bodies and our houses and possessions must be cleansed

Stop and Smell

Normally, I'm a very healthy person. I can usually get through the stresses and strains of losing sleep and working hard and being exposed to varieties of germs my children have a way of bringing home. In fact, until this past fall I had taken delight in boasting that I hadn't spent a full day in bed since the day I was married (excluding those hospital-imposed days of rest after each of our babies arrived).

Somehow things have been different this winter! For the second time in a little more than a month my head pounds with the pressure of a sinus infection. My eyes water, my nose feels stuffed up and my throat is sore. Food seems absolutely tasteless and I can't smell a thing.

Now that my "smeller" is out of commission, I have begun to realize how valuable it is to me. Ordinarily it keeps me informed as to when one of the babies needs a change of diapers. I can always tell if the meat I buy is really fresh by the way it smells. Sometimes my nose warns

daily, so must our hearts be cleansed from the filthiness of daily sin.

David prayed, "Wash me throughly from mine iniquity, and cleanse me from my sin.... Create in me a clean heart, O God, and renew a right spirit within me" (Ps. 51:2). And so, even though we must be occupied with the dirt we see around us, let us not forget the daily cleansing of the heart which every Christian requires.

me that the gasjet on my stove is not working right and that the fire did not light when the gas was turned on. Occasionally (but more often than I care to admit) my nose tells me that the potatoes have already boiled dry and are about to burn! Just last week I discovered by the aroma which filled my bedroom that little Donnie had been having fun with my skin cream!

There are so many pleasant things our noses do for us. A fat brown turkey roasting in the oven tastes twice as good because the smell gets our tastebuds tingling even before we get a bite. A rose is lovely, not only because of its velvety, glowing petals but because it also exudes the sweetness of its perfume, and fills the air with its fragrance. I always enjoy the smell of burning leaves, the musty smell of old books, the scent of new leather shoes, the smell of the earth after a summer shower. And is there anything sweeter than the smell of a clean baby?

Our sense of smell, of all the five senses, seems to be the most easily jaded by constant exposure to any one impression. For instance, if I should happen to wear perfume, I am likely to smell it very strongly for the first hour but gradually I become completely unaware of it, even though others who come near me may still notice the fragrance.

Sometimes a fire, started in some hidden part of a building, may go completely unnoticed until it is out of control because the occupants have become gradually de-sensitized to the odor of the smoke through constant, though subtle exposure to its smell.

I remember a little town we used to pass through on the way to my grandfather's farm, where some kind of chemical was manufactured. The smell of the whole town was so terrible I often wondered how people could stand to live there day in and day out. My mother reminded me that we noticed it because we were not used to it, but that the people who lived there had become so accustomed to it that they hardly knew the town had an odor.

Sin, unperfumed by fancy names and elaborate excuses, is an evil-smelling, deadly gas. A clear conscience (like a clear nose) will warn the alert individual that something must be done. The source of the gas must be cut off; the air must be cleared. Any time the heart ignores the warnings and pleadings of the conscience, the sensitivity to sin diminishes. The reeking stench of sin may go on and on but somehow the distaste is gone; the dulled conscience no longer warns.

Perhaps you need to sharpen your spiritual senses. May it never be true of you (or me) that our sin no longer disturbs us. Better to notice the foul odor and get rid of it than to learn to live with it.

Stop and smell!

Bright Windows

Isn't it interesting how so many of our ideas and ambitions find their basis in little, almost insignificant impressions?

During college days, when going to and from school I used to walk past a particular home which always held delight and fascination for me. The house was on a corner, rather close to the street and the curtains in the living room and kitchen were always open. It is not surprising that the lady who lived there never seemed to mind that passers-by could see the interior of her home. At dusk on a snowy winter's day the warm, glowing pictures her windows presented were enough to make any lingering batchelor head joyfully for the altar, and any wandering mother's boy quicken his step toward home.

The orderly kitchen was bright in yellow and white and the windowsill was decked with geraniums and African violets. Through the large picture window in the living room, it was easy to see the tasteful accumulation of pictures and books and lamps softly lit and comfortable-looking chairs and a huge grand piano. Sometimes when I passed by the lady was teaching piano lessons and I often thought how pleasant it must be to be teaching (or to be learning) in those surroundings. Sometimes I could see the lady of the house busy in her kitchen and I could almost smell the delicious things I felt certain she was concocting.

I thoroughly enjoyed my college days but I never passed that house without thinking that the fun and freedom of school days were surely nothing compared to the bliss of having a home and family and doing some creative work like teaching young people music or art. Sometimes even now, in the late afternoon of a busy day, the memory of those pleasant windows helps me to make the extra effort to brighten up the view through my own front window by a little last-minute house-straightening and light-ing of lamps and freshening up of myself and the children. If that lady only knew what her lovely windows did for me--how happy she would be!

Now that I have a home and a family of my

own, I know that not everything shows through the living room window (or any other window, for that matter). A casual glance through the front window does not inform the passer-by that some part of the plumbing is not working right or that the delicious dinner in the oven is about to spoil because the husband is late com-ing home from work. And it could be that the lady sitting so patiently by the piano listening to some little boy stumble through an unprac-ticed rendition of "Country Gardens" would give anything if there were no necessity for helping the family budget by teaching piano lessons. Or perhaps she is worried about a sick husband or her own child who may not be doing well in school.

Bright, pleasant front windows are fine for pleasing the eye of the passer-by and for set-ting house-keeping examples for young girls to follow, but they certainly do not tell the whole story.

In our Christian experience we all meet those marvelous people who "have every-thing." We gaze with envy on the fortunate few who seem to have received more than their share of talent, opportunity, good looks, spar-

Questions! Questions! Questions!

This morning as I was making oatmeal-raisin cookies Carol and Jimmy and Donnie climbed up on chairs to watch. What confusion they added to a usually simple task! Stirring, reading a recipe, keeping little fingers out of the bowl and answering a dozen unrelated questions all at the same time took a mite of doing, I'll tell you! Oh, the questions! How can children find so many things to ask about?

I found myself laughing (through gritted teeth) at the new feminist movement which declares that the job of being a wife and mother does not allow a woman to exercise her full mental capabilities. Well, I don't know about you, but I'm afraid my opportunities for exercising my mental facilities have already overreached my ability to find all the answers. None of my children are in school yet but I am finding that I have to be a theologian, a scientist, a mechanic, an artist and a dozen kinds of engineer just to keep up with their everyday questions. "Mommy, why don't horses have knees on their

kling personality, friends and even "spirituality." Their "window to the world" is bright and shining and we feel a little piqued that the Lord didn't see fit to distribute His gifts more equally. We have no way of seeing the extra responsibilities and burdens and temptations that go with the gifts. A house with a shining living room must also have a broom closet; a pleasant kitchen with pleasant smells must also have tools for scrubbing dirty pots and pans. Then let us not fret if our gifts are less spectacular than those of some other Christian. Perhaps our burdens and problems are not as heavy either. The Lord has given us the responsibility for our OWN front windows. Let's make them bright and beautiful for Him!

"Let your light so shine before men, that they may see your good works, and glorify your Father which is in heaven."--Matt. 5:16.

back legs like elephants do?" "What makes the wind blow?" "How can Jesus be in Heaven and in my heart too?" "What makes a car go?" "Why aren't there any more giants?" "What keeps the big buildings from falling over?" "Do mommy animals talk to their babies?" "What does Grandma Sandberg do in Heaven?" "Why can't I fly with my arms like birds do?"

Now I ask you--if answering the questions children ask doesn't strain a mother's mental capacity, what does?

But those aren't the only questions I have to find the answers for (bad grammar but profound truth). It takes some rather careful figuring for me to buy a week's supply of groceries for a family of six on a limited budget and get through the checkout counter without having to put something back on the shelves. And nearly all housewives learn some little tricks for making faulty appliances work, repairing broken lamps, clearing sluggish plumbing and mending furniture. For instance, I discovered just last week that the temperamental agitator of my washing machine would always work if I remembered to slam the lid shut once or twice!

Life seems to be a process of trying to find

192

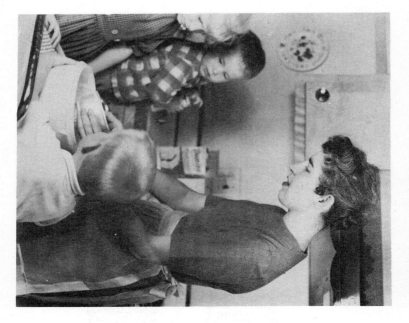

answers and solutions to our problems. Our hearts are full of questions: "Why do Christians have to suffer?" "How can I be the kind of mother I ought to be?" "Why can't I win my children to the Lord?" "How can we pay these bills?" "When will my husband be saved?" We tug at the hem of God's garments like little children, pleading for answers.

What a comfort it is to know that God is not hampered by any human inadequacies. He is never too busy to care. He is not frustrated by problems too big to handle. He has ALL the answers!

"If any of you lack wisdom, let him ask of God, that giveth to all men liberally, and upbraideth not." --James 1:5.

A Bad Day for Donnie

This simply has not been little eighteen-month-old Donnie's day!

Almost from the moment his little feet touched the floor this morning he has been in trouble. What a continual round we have had of spankings, scoldings, and exasperated sighs (mine, not his)! He has teased his big sister and brother by snatching their toys and running away with them as fast as he could; he has squeezed the baby until he cried. He has been on top of every piece of furniture and into every drawer and cabinet. He has messed with his food, tracked the floor with mud, and written on the walls. I won't even go into the things he broke, the things he spilled, the tears, the pouting, the angry little face and the other little contributions he made to a rather worse-than-average day! The final straw came when he got into the peanut butter jar and then messed up Daddy's best (and only) hat.

But little sinners--like big ones--really do

not find any joy in being bad, and Donnie was not happy long without love and forgiveness in my arms. He hasn't learned to say "I'm sorry" but the tearful kiss he gave me after every spanking and the sweet way he patted my face at bedtime told me that he didn't enjoy being alienated from Mommy's favor by his wrong-doing. I am always distressed when my children sin, but I probably don't have to convince you that I keep on loving them just the same. I may be angry or disappointed or just plain disgusted with Donnie's naughtiness, but he is always dear and precious to me.

In my daily Bible reading through the Old Testament I have noticed again the terrible recurrence of the complaints and backsliding of the children of Israel. If I hadn't already known the way the story would end, I would have surely thought the Lord was going to give them up as hopeless long before He got them to the promised land. How sad the story is, and yet how typical of the whole human race—sin, punishment, repentance, forgiveness and then sin again to be repeated over and over. What infinite patience and mercy and longsuffering on the part of God that He never turns a deaf ear to the heart pleading for forgiveness!

Just the other day a lady called me on the phone to ask some advice about a matter. She said that the Lord didn't love her anymore and wouldn't tell her what she ought to do. She was so frustrated and miserable, she had almost decided life wasn't worth living. I assured her that the Lord never stops loving His children and that she could have perfect confidence of His love and care by (1) seeking His forgiveness for any known sin, by (2) daily reading the Word with the determination to obey whatever it commanded, by (3) trusting God to do everything He has promised to do. When we do wrong, we may FEEL that the Lord no longer loves us, but His Word promises us that He does. Like Donnie, we can come back for forgiveness after every spanking and be assured that God will take us in His forgiving arms.

He loves you still, how long His love has waited,
As in your sinful way you wandered on,
You wounded Him, Ah yes! you crucified Him;
But still He loves and seeks the erring one.

A Mother's Instinct

I am always amazed when I stop to consider how wonderfully the body is made. What infinite wisdom it took to put together this maze of bones, nerves, organs, muscles and glands to form a creature made in the image of God. It would be marvelous if God's creation ended with the formation of the frame, with the mechanism of the various organs of the body, but God didn't stop there. Just think how much more intricate is the personality, the emotional and mental processes that make us behave the way we do. What a delicate balance there is in each of us of various emotions and feelings--reserve and aggressiveness, capacities to love and to hate, of ambition and contentment, of desires to please ourselves and still win the favor of others. And how marvelous are the instincts God gives to help us do some things naturally which we could not perhaps be taught to do.

Take, for instance, the child-consciousness which seems to come, in normal cases, when a woman gives birth to a baby. I remember so clearly the first night I spent in the hospital after my oldest child, Carol, was born. I was in a place where every need of my baby was being taken care of by others. I hadn't changed a diaper, bathed, fed or "burped" my baby, and yet when I heard a baby cry in the night, I woke with a start thinking, "That must be my baby." I had been in places before where babies cried at night but there was no sudden wakefulness, no quickening of the heart. That child-consciousness came when I became a mother; not before.

My mother says that although her babies are all grown and have homes of their own, she never hears a little child call "Mommy!" without turning quickly to see if it is one of her own little girls.

My husband and I laugh at each other if we ever have occasion to be riding in the car without our children. At every stop sign or turn in the road we both automatically fling out an arm to protect the little one who isn't there! In fact, I sometimes have to fight down the impulse, when riding alone to cry out, "Look, children, see the horses?" I am so used to

watching for things that will amuse my children in the car.

Last week my two older children were at a Little Tot's Bible Class and my two babies were taking naps. I had thought it might be a good time to get lots of work done but I found myself pausing every now and then to hear the voices of children playing, forgetting that mine were not at home. I was so distracted by listening for children who were not there it was nice to have them home again so I could get my work done!

A mother may have a thousand things on her mind, but the softest cry or sound of a child in need can make her thoughts leap instantly to her own children. . . .

What a blessed thing it would be if we had the same consciousness of the Lord Jesus as we do of our children. If we were always aware of Him, always seeking His fellowship, always concerned to please Him, then it would not be so difficult for us to fulfill that biblical command, "Pray without ceasing" (I Thess. 5:17). It isn't unusual for one to wake up in the morning feeling the sweetness of the Lord's presence if the last waking thoughts the night before were directed toward Him. It isn't difficult to reach the Saviour in sudden times of stress if in our moments of peace and joy we have talked with Him and shared His fellowship.

Does it seem an impossible command that we are told to 'pray always' (Eph. 6:18)--to be always within a prayer's length of the throne of God? Ask a woman who has borne children and fed them and taught them to walk and talk and nursed them in sickness--ask her if it is difficult for her to remember that she is a mother. No, just as there is an instinct which makes a woman constantly aware of her children, so there ought to be a holy awareness in the heart of every Christian which makes prayer a continual thing--a telephone line to Heaven which requires no dialing and no delay.

"How Long Will It Be?"

For days and days our little Carol had been looking forward to our trip to Moline. Every night before she would go to bed she would always ask the same question: "Now how many nights do I have to go to sleep before we leave, Mommy?" And there were lots more questions, too: "How long will we get to stay?" "Will I get to play with all my cousins there?" "Will we go to church there?" "Will Aunt Minner stay home from work so I can help her clean house?"

And my, what preparation there had to be! For once, Carol was only too happy to have her hair washed and curled. Usually she dreads the washing and brushing of her long blond curls. Her head is sensitive and Mommy always seems to find the tangles! But she felt she could stand any kind of discomfort, in prospect of a trip to see her beloved Aunt Minner and Uncle Ray. What fun it was, planning what would go in the suitcases, deciding what she would wear. And how eager she was to have Aunt Minner see the new patent leather Sunday shoes. She played as usual, slept as usual, and ate as usual, but always in the forefront of her mind was the thought that soon she would be going to Moline.

When we finally did get into the car with all the paraphernalia necessary when one travels with little children, a new series of questions began. "Now how long will it be, Mommy?" "Now how far do we have to go?" "Are we almost there?" "Now how many minutes?" As the familiar landmarks began to come into view, all the children began to squeal and dance with delight. Just think--we were almost THERE!

Though I smiled indulgently at the impatience and eagerness of the children, I remembered a little wistfully how I felt as a child when we made trips back to Texas to visit all our friends and relatives there. The thousand miles of wearying highway travel in a crowded car were nothing compared to the joy of being again with those we loved. One year we even had to forego the delight of decorating a Christmas tree and having our usual celebration in snow-covered Illinois so that we could leave in time to

have Christmas with Grandpa and Grandma Cooke. As much as I loved all the preparation for the Christmas holidays, I was more than willing to do without that so that we could spend the time with those we loved. It was all a matter of values. We were certainly willing to give up the good for the best.

I can't help thinking how different life would be for us if we felt the same eagerness and anticipation for Heaven as Carol felt at the prospect of going to Moline. How wonderful it would be if our last thought at night were always, "Perhaps tonight He will come to take me home" or at morningtime our first thought would be, "Oh, if only this would be the day I could see Jesus!" Of course there will be no thrill of anticipation, no expectation of joy, if there is no preparedness. If we have no sheaves to bring, then it is natural that we would feel dread rather than joy at the thought of meeting Jesus. And if we have become so preoccupied with the cares of this life that we have forgotten how sweet His fellowship is, then that is sadder still.

No wonder we are so easily discouraged, so easily bogged down by all the petty frustrations and problems of living! We have forgotten what Heaven will mean. We need to read again the promise: ". . . Behold, the tabernacle of God is with men, and he will dwell with them, and they shall be his people, and God himself shall be with them, and be their God. And God shall wipe away all tears from their eyes; and there shall be no more death, neither sorrow, nor crying, neither shall there be any more pain: for the former things are passed away" (Rev. 21:4, 5).

O Lord Jesus, how long, how long
Ere we shout the glad song,
Christ returneth! Hallelujah!
Hallelujah! Amen.

Rich Man -- Poor Man

My husband and I don't get much time for the usual kinds of outings enjoyed by married couples but we do have lots of fun together. One of our favorite means of achieving "togetherness" is to prop up our feet, surround ourselves with plenty of reading material, fill a couple of bowls with ice cream (with nuts and chocolate sauce added to fatten up my 145-lb. husband), and then to spend the evening interrupting each other's reading to make comments on whatever it is we ourselves are reading. Of course it means we often get into discussions about the reading material and that's where the "togetherness" comes in!

Last night when we were pursuing just such a pastime my husband let out a long low whistle of disbelief and so I peeked over his shoulder to see what amazed him so. He was reading an article in a current magazine about an exclusive store for women in New York City which has the richest clientele in the world. According to the author of the article, the store has at least 50 regular customers who spend more than $80,000 a year there and a great deal more when they feel a need for new fur coats beside. "How in the world," I asked, "can one individual spend over $80,000 a year on clothes?" We jokingly tried to imagine ourselves spending that much money on the luxuries of life but we just couldn't think of enough things we wanted, to use up that amount! When all is said and done, how much difference can there be between a well-made $20 dress and a designer-produced $20,000 one?

Without even a taste of sour grapes, Don and I reminded ourselves that happiness for a Christian has nothing--absolutely nothing to do with money. What a relaxing, comfortable thought that is!

Did you ever realize that no matter how many clothes a person owns he can still wear only one outfit at a time? No matter how much money an individual can afford to spend on food, his body can hold only a certain amount. Even the quality of food is not necessarily improved with the cost. Many a man with modest income eats as well as the rich because he has a wife who is a skilled and careful cook. Good literature is not more enjoyable because one is rich, nor

is it less enjoyable because one is poor. A comfortable chair is not necessarily softer for a rich man than it is for a poor man. A man is not automatically healthier because he is rich. The brilliant blue sky, the glow of a summer sunset, the delicate yellow of a spring crocus-- all display their beauty to the rich and poor alike. The poor may love and beloved as free-ly as the rich.

Lest I be misunderstood, let me remind you that to have an ungrateful heart is a sin, just as having a covetous heart would be a sin. Every comfort of life, every little luxury and pleasure provided by a loving Heavenly Father ought to be received with thankfulness. The Apostle Paul spoke very wisely when he said: " . . . I have learned, in whatsoever state I am, therewith to be content. I know both how to be abased, and I know how to abound: everywhere and in all things I am instructed both to be full and to be hungry, both to abound and to suffer need. I can do all things through Christ which strength-eneth me."

Being poor is a happy condition if it is ac-companied with a sweet trust in a God who can and does foresee our every need. Wealth is wonderful when it is used to demonstrate that God loves to bring prosperity to His own diligent servants. Better still is the state of being neither too rich nor too poor where neither want of money nor excess of it tempts us to discouragement or to greed. The Holy Spirit, again through the Apostle Paul, gives us this formula for finding "the best things in life":

"Rejoice in the Lord alway: and again I say, Rejoice. Let your moderation be known unto all men. The Lord is at hand. Be careful for nothing: but in everything by prayer and supplication with thanksgiving let your requests be made known unto God. And the peace of God, which passeth all understanding, shall keep your hearts and minds through Christ Jesus."
--Phil. 4:4-7.

Mother's Day

How well I remember that first Mother's Day after our first child was born. Our baby had arrived prematurely the previous December and had lived for only an hour. When Mother's Day came there was a special service in the church and all the mothers were supposed to stand while a rose was pinned to the dress of each. There were white-haired mothers whose children had long since left the home-nest. There were mothers with growing children gathered around them. There were brand new mothers with shining eyes, proudly holding tiny little red-faced babies.

I didn't stand. I had no little ones around me to prove that I was a mother. In fact, I had never had the joy of fulfilling a single mother's task for that little one who was now in Heaven with the Lord Jesus. I had never diapered him, rocked him to sleep, fed him or done any of the jobs a mother does joyfully for her children. But still, I felt I was a mother as completely as any woman who stood.

Sometimes now, when I feel overwhelmed with the pressure of taking care of the four children which God has given me since, I remember the longing I felt at that particular time.

Mother's Day is here again. Some mothers will be served their once-a-year breakfast in bed; some will receive lovely bouquets of flowers; others will begiven boxes of candy. There will be sweet Mother's Day kisses from little children, and notes of gratitude from grown-up children who are far away.

Perhaps there is a woman reading this page who will not be wearing a rose this week to indicate that she is a mother. Perhaps·there is an unfulfilled longing for children which those who are nearest and dearest would never suspect. It may be that life seems wasted and useless because there have been no children to grace the home and occupy the hours.

Well it IS a thrilling and wonderful privilege to give birth to a little baby, but that is not necessarily the highest fulfillment life has to offer. Many a mother whose grown son has brought heartache and disgrace will tell you that. And even in good homes, children are sometimes ungrateful and careless toward the mother who bore them.

If you long for children, then win souls! When one begets spiritual children it always turns out right. True, there may be heartache as you see the new Christian struggling with the old nature which still dwells within, but there is a sense of fulfillment which no other occupation can equal. Just think how much sweeter Heaven will be if there are many "children" to present to the Saviour.

Last week a young fellow came to my house selling magazines. He had been reared in a Catholic orphanage and hoped to go on to college by earning a scholarship. I told him I had no use for more magazines but that I had something good to tell him. To my surprise, he listened quietly and patiently while I went through the plan of salvation from the book of Romans (the method taught by Dr. Jack Hyles in his book, LET'S GO SOUL WINNING!) and then afterwards he haltingly and tearfully asked the Lord Jesus to come into his heart. About that time my husband came home from work and I was just thrilled to present my new "spir-

"itual child" as I have been to show off each of my own earthly babies.

A happy Mother's Day to each of you, and may your life be rich with the joy of bringing forth many children!

"He maketh the barren woman to keep house, and to be a joyful mother of children. Praise ye the Lord." —Ps. 113:9.

The Face You Wear

Do you ever wake up, give yourself a good look in the mirror and then wish you could crawl back into bed?

Deep down inside me, I usually think of myself as a perpetual twenty-one-year-old girl. I hope that doesn't sound like some kind of self-delusion. Of course I have a great deal more responsibility than I did when I was actually twenty-one, and less freedom, but I feel just as lively and on the whole I enjoy the same things I did then. The shock always comes when I look in the mirror and see that my face is obviously that of a thirty-three-year-old woman and my rapidly graying hair sometimes gives people the impression that I am older than that!

It is almost funny how subtly nature makes her mark on the human face. The firm cheek begins to sag a little. The eyes get a tired look. Fine lines around the mouth and upon the forehead begin to etch themselves deeper and deeper.

Just the other day I read an article about a

lady who felt a great need for a facelift because a severe illness had left her looking much older than her age. After the expensive and painful operation was over, the doctor told her that the best thing she could do to keep her new face in shape was to "look happy."

In a generation of women almost swallowed up in an overemphasis on cosmetics and beauty aids, it sounds strange to hear someone say that the way to a beautiful face is to "look happy." If we are to believe the magazine ads and the TV commercials, beauty of face is acquired by an expensive array of cosmetics for the hair, the eyes, the mouth, and the skin. There are always "before and after" pictures to show what a great improvement the latest beauty preparation can make over nature.

Lest I be misunderstood, let me hasten to say that this is not a tirade against cosmetics. I am only intending to say that cosmetics are no substitute for the beauty that comes from within.

There is an old saying that a woman is not responsible for her face when she is sixteen; that is the face nature gave her. She IS responsible for the kind of face she has when she is sixty for that is the face she herself has carved

by the way she has lived. Many a woman with rather ordinary features has a special beauty in her mature years because her eyes shine with the law of kindness and her pleasant expression has been formed by contentment and good humor.

On the other hand, there are women--considered beautiful in their girlhood, who have so lived for themselves in selfishness and distrust, that their mature faces seem fixed in a permanent pout.

I know a woman--an extremely plain woman, whose face is so radiant when she speaks or smiles that one forgets how homely she really is. She is a wonderfully gifted woman, interested in many activities, and she is much in demand as a guest because she is so much fun to have around.

Have you heard that beauty is only skin deep? Don't believe it! Perhaps there is a regularity of feature and a happy arrangement of form which is skin deep only, but the kind of beauty that lasts and lasts and lasts, comes from within.

"Likewise, ye wives, be in subjection to

your own husbands; that, if any obey not the word, they also may without the word be won by the conversation of the wives; While they behold your chaste conversation coupled with fear. Whose adorning let it not be that outward adorning of plaiting the hair, and of wearing of gold, or of putting on of apparel; But let it be the hidden man of the heart, in that which is not corruptible, even the ornament of a meek and quiet spirit, which is in the sight of God of great price."--I Pet. 3:1-4.

"Favour is deceitful and beauty is vain: but a woman that feareth the Lord, she shall be praised."--Prov. 31:30.

The Storm That Didn't Come

This morning the weather predictions on the radio were pretty grim. The commentator stated that there would be thundershowers, hail and possibly tornados by late afternoon.

In spite of the weather warnings the sun came out in glorious brightness and with it, the little children came out to play. Housewives got their Monday washes on the line extra early so that the clothes would be dry before the rain came.

Sure enough, by noon the wind was beginning to whip itself into a fury, plastering bits of paper and grass against the west side of the house. Clouds began to appear in the southwest and rapidly filled the sky like a bowl of cream being whipped into giant swirls of foam. "Oh, look, Mommy," my five-year-old daughter squealed, "the grass looks like its flying away!" And indeed it did.

By two o'clock, the neighborhood was all set for the threatened storm. Not a garment hung on any line; not a child was seen outdoors--only an anxious mother darted out to retrieve a tricycle left on a neighbor's lawn. Little faces peered from front windows, watching for the storm to come.

By now the sky was so dark we had to turn on the lights at our house in order to see our work. Far in the distance the thunder rolled and our radio crackled with storm-static. I remembered belatedly that I really should have made certain the door to the tool shed was fastened securely so the wind could not blow it open. I wondered if the lid to the garbage can would blow away as it had last year.

Soon the rain came. Not the hail and slashing rains which we had expected--with sparkling lightning and deafening thunder--only a light sprinkling which barely covered the streets.

Within five minutes it was all over. The trees stood in such eerie stillness it was difficult to believe that only a few moments earlier they were bending and twisting with the force of the wind. No doubt the storm did touch down somewhere near us, but for us it disappeared before it arrived. There was no hail, no torna-

do--nothing to prove we had ALMOST had a storm.

Sometimes, under the conviction of plain preaching, or in the fervor of a revival meeting, or through a deep study of the Word of God, we make holy vows to serve the Lord with new zeal. Like the lashing wind of a gathering storm we fly into action, determined to win lost souls, zealous to do anything God tells us to do. The world watches us expectantly, waiting to see what will come of all our thunder and rolling clouds.

Then, just when the Lord is about to send a down-pouring of His blessing on our work and ministry, we get discouraged, or we get too busy to read the Bible and to pray. Suddenly, without any apparent reason, the wind dies down to a whisper and our opportunities to do something great for God are over. Our worldly friends sit back and say bitterly, "Well, I didn't think it would last!" For all our grand and tumultuous beginnings to win our lost loved ones, many of us give up too soon, just when the Holy Spirit is about to bring the refreshing rain of His power and influence.

". . .Prove me now herewith, saith the Lord

of hosts, if I will not open you the windows of heaven, and pour you out a blessing, that there shall not be room enough to receive it." --Mal. 3:10.

What Kind of Shoes Are the Shoes You Wear?

One of my favorite books as a school girl was about a young lady who always wore flat practical shoes because she loved to tramp through woods and mountains. People were always asking her, "What kind of shoes are the shoes you wear?" She usually convinced them that they ought to wear sensible shoes and go hiking in the mountains too!

Now I'm all for practical shoes when it comes to climbing mountains (or for ironing and washing dishes) but I enjoy the pretty kind too. Before we were married my husband bought me a pair of beautiful red cobra shoes as a Christmas gift. I was not there when he bought them and have no idea how he knew my size, but the fit was perfect. They were lovely, expensive shoes and I felt very queenly when I wore them.

Now that we have a family of four children, the budget does not allow for too many fancy shoes. Just about the time we think we are through with the shoe store for a while, we discover that our fast-growing little girl is already crowding the toes of her not-so-old Sunday shoes. Jimmy, being a rather typical little boy, sometimes scuffs his shoes so badly he wears them out before he is even ready to go to the next size. Before we know it, little Don will be ready for regular "boy shoes" (as compared with high-top toddler shoes) and baby Mark will need hard soles for walking. It's a rather perpetual thing—trying to keep a family of children well-shod.

My husband Don helps to level out our shoe budget a little because he takes such good care of his shoes. He still has one pair of shoes he bought before we were married (eight years ago) and although they have been half-soled more than once, they still look nice. He always remembers to wear rubbers in the rain and he keeps his shoes well-polished, using some tried and true method he learned during his army days.

Isn't it interesting how fascinated children are by grown-up shoes? Our little ones love to bury themselves in our closet and re-appear wearing their parents' shoes. Little Donnie sometimes digs out his Daddy's heaviest shoes

and proudly clomps all over the house until the sheer weight of the shoes wears him out. Carol usually chooses something of mine in shiny patent leather, or with very high heels. Then with her little feet all "squnched up" in the toes of my big shoes she wobbles around, trying very hard to look like Mommy.

Now it is one thing, seeing my children struggling to wear my ordinary, earthly shoes, but it is quite another thing to see them putting on my spiritual shoes as well. It is an awesome thing to see how perfectly a little girl may imitate her mother's way of doing something or to hear her use an expression or manner of speech which she has almost subconsciously learned from her mother.

How eager little children are to walk in their parents' shoes, and how quick they are to copy what they see. They hear the critical tone their parents use when discussing friends or neighbors. They are aware of the sullen look of discontent. They sense the rebellion a woman feels toward her husband. They see the sudden anger. They know when a mother or father is careless about spiritual things; slovenly about prayer and Bible reading. Whether we intend it to be so, or not, our children will become, for the most part, the kind of people we ourselves are.

May God give us the grace to walk in such a way we won't be ashamed to see our children wearing our spiritual shoes!

"See then that ye walk circumspectly, not as fools, but as wise, Redeeming the time, because the days are evil. Wherefore be ye not unwise, but understanding what the will of the Lord is."--Eph. 5:15-17.

What kind of shoes are the shoes you wear?

When Children Pray

If I ever write a book about the things I have learned from my childrens' prayers, it will probably be a volume three inches thick! What a simplicity and honesty there is in a child's prayer, and what faith accompanies its trip to the throne of God! At our family prayers I am always glad to have the children pray before me because their praying helps me to know how I ought to pray!

In the first place, my children ENJOY talking to the Lord. They use a conversational tone as they would when speaking to a very dear friend. The other night Jimmy was thanking Jesus for the new bunk beds and he ended his prayer this way: "... 'n you know what? Carol's bed is way up high and she gets to climb a ladder!... and thank you for everything. Amen."

When it was Carol's turn to pray she continued the little tete-a-tete with the Lord which Jimmy had started. She began her prayer by saying, "Well, the first thing I want to tell you is that Linda is very sick and she needs You to make her well . . ."

Certainly the Lord is not displeased with the informality of a child's prayer. In fact, I rather suspect that Jesus' disciples tried to shoo away the little children who came to Him because they thought He would not care about their childish interests and needs. But Jesus did care then, and He surely cares now. Perhaps if we could discard all the meaningless phrases that obscure our real needs and desires when we pray, then the Lord could answer our prayers as He so often does for little children.

To my children, prayer is never the last resort in any need. It is the FIRST step toward settling any problem. If someone is sick, I am likely to call the doctor first and pray afterward. If something is lost, I look for it first, and THEN pray that it will be found. If there is a problem to be solved, I work at it and work at it and THEN I ask the Lord for the answer. If there is a heavy burden to be borne, I grit my teeth and lug it onto my own shoulders until it gets too heavy for me and THEN I ask the Lord to carry it for me.

Not so with my children. To them--and to the Lord, incidentally--the obvious, logical way is to PRAY FIRST. What time we waste using our puny little resources when we could have all the resources of the God of Heaven at our disposal!

Because my children have such a good speaking acquaintance with the Lord, they never need to go to prayer pretending to be something they are not. Once my little girl prayed with tears running down her face, "Dear Jesus, I told a lie and that was very bad. I don't want to be a liar." Now if I had gone to the Lord confessing such a sin, I might have hesitated to actually call myself a liar. I would have preferred a more pious way of putting it, such as ". . . I said something which I probably ought not to have said. . ." No wonder the publican went down to his house justified, rather than the other!

When my children pray, they expect answers. Sometimes I almost have to bite my tongue lest I weaken my children's faith by intimating that God cannot or will not fulfill His Word. Occasionally a mother says, "But what if my children pray for something and then God doesn't answer?" My reply would be this: We don't have to make alibis for God. We ought to teach our children what the Bible says about prayer so that they CAN have their prayers answered and we ought to encourage them to pray about everything. Furthermore, we ought to expect and regularly receive answers to prayers ourselves. Beyond that, it is up to the Lord. He will do exactly what He has promised to do.

"Ask, and it shall be given you; seek, and ye shall find; knock, and it shall be opened unto you: For everyone that asketh receiveth; and he that seeketh findeth; and to him that knocketh it shall be opened."--Matt. 7:7, 8.

Measles and Other Diseases

Childhood illnesses are always a matter of concern to parents. We do whatever is in our power to prevent those which are preventable and to make those which are not preventable as easy as possible. We see that our children get shots for whooping cough, diptheria, tetanus and polio when they are very small, and then we have them vaccinated for smallpox at least by the time they are ready for school. We try to keep them from getting other communicable diseases when they are less than a year old because we know the complications are usually more serious for very young children. Sometimes, even with care, our children pick up the germs of something which happens to be "going around," and in larger families that means the disease will most likely spread to more than one member of the household.

At our house, for instance, we have just finished a bout with the measles. What a time we have had with fever and sore throats and shots and spots and sleepless nights and fussy children! And what a relief it has been to see the eyes brighten as the spots faded and to see the appetites return.

Actually, I should be grateful that we had to fight only half a battle. Carol and Jimmy had already had measles when they were small and so when little Don broke out we knew Baby Mark would be the only child in danger of getting them. And fortunately, we were able to get a gamma globulin shot for him so that he would only have a light case.

As any mother knows, the worst part of a case of measles is always the period of time before the spots begin to appear. Little Don went for a week with a high fever and nothing we did would keep it below 103 degrees for very long. Finally the doctor gave penicillin to help the inflamed ears and throat. The poor little fellow was so dosed up with cough syrup and aspirin and antibiotics that he dreaded seeing Mommy approach with a bottle of any kind. When at last the deep red rash began to appear, we all sighed with relief because we knew the worst would soon be over.

If there is anything nice about a case of measles, it is the permanent immunity one gains

by suffering through it one time. How nice it is to know we can now take our children to church and other public places without a second thought as to whether they will "catch" the measles again.

Sin is a fatal disease. It has been communicated to every child born and has contaminated the whole human race. There is no toxin one can take to keep from becoming infected. All the sweet-smelling salves we may use-- education, culture, refinement, even human righteousness--may help to hide the rash but they do not heal the disease.

Thank God, there is a cure. Though sin may blight our bodies, our purposes, and our dreams, we do not have to die of the disease. All we need to do is to turn to the dear Sin-bearer who took all the awful infection of sin in His own body and gave His blood as a cure for every sin-sick heart.

Are you looking for healing from the curse of sin? Then look to Jesus and accept His once-and-for-all cure. He is the Great Physician.

"But unto you that fear my name shall the Sun

of righteousness arise with healing in his wings . . . . " --Mal. 4:2.

"For God so loved the world, that he gave his only begotten Son, that whosoever believeth in him should not perish, but have everlasting life." --John 3:16.

Just Like Mommy!

Sunday night suppers at our house are very informal. Usually no one is very hungry after a late Sunday dinner and my husband, Don, doesn't like to eat much, anyway, before the evening service where he will be busy leading the music and working with the choir. The children usually ask for a bowl of cereal, unless they see me eating one of my favorite snacks--ordinary bread or crackers broken up in a glass of milk! Actually, I don't know that they really like bread and milk. It is just that they think it is so much fun to eat whatever they see Mommy eat!

My sister once got so tired of eating the economical foods which her budget required (in the process of raising four hungry boys and girls!) that she decided to splurge just once and buy some real extravagant delicacy which she and her husband could enjoy. She finally decided on artichokes--two small servings-- thinking that surely her children would not be interested in such strange fare. But of course, when the children saw their parents eating with such relish, they decided THEY liked artichokes too, and so THAT delicacy did not go far. Later the parents tried the same thing with shrimp, only to discover that shrimp was suddenly their offsprings' favorite dish.

Strange, isn't it, how strongly we are affected by what other people do? A girl who sees her mother smoke usually thinks nothing of doing it herself, even though the mother may declare a thousand times that she wishes she had never begun. A boy who is used to seeing liquor in the house will often buy his first can of beer before he is of age, even though he does it without his father's knowledge or wish. Pleadings and threats are practically of no worth whatever as compared with the power of an example set by a father or mother.

In homes where parents are constantly criticizing pastors and teachers, or joking about breaking small laws, the children will NEARLY ALWAYS have contempt for authority. Children have a way of seeing beyond our pious affections, and they have a tendency to be what they see in us, whether good or bad.

I notice in my own children that if they hear

me say once or twice, "I wish we could afford to buy . . ." or "I surely would like to have a new . . ." then their little "wanters" start to get busy too! Pretty soon I hear one of them say, "Mommy, I wish I had a new doll (or toy truck or wagon)." If that should happen too often, the children would soon start thinking that life and happiness consisted of "things"--and that would be a terrible legacy to leave a child!

My little niece Linda is only four but she is trying very hard to win her little neighborhood friends to the Lord. That is not surprising because her daddy is a preacher and he spends some time nearly every day trying to win someone to the Lord. There is almost never a week when he does not win at least two and sometimes there are as many as eight or ten who are saved because of his personal witnessing. Linda is so used to hearing her father pray for lost souls and seeing his happy smile when someone is saved, that she naturally wants to be a soul winner too.

What are your "wants" in life? Are they the things you would wish for your childern to have and to be?

Talk

It is a standard joke among men that women would rather talk than do anything else. One husband I know loves to tease his wife about spending all day "slaving over a hot telephone!"

Perhaps men do not get together in "clubby" little groups quite as much as women do, but it is a fact that everybody needs someone to talk to. Farmers gather at the farm implement store, businessmen have conventions, housewives talk over the back fence, business girls gather around the water cooler, worldly people sometimes get together at the local bar, and Christians linger at the door of the church to "visit" a little. Even preachers need a chance to talk about their problems and situations and so they get together for "fellowship meetings" or "associational meetings."

My husband has an aunt and uncle who regularly visit an old people's home because they have found that old folks are usually starved for a little bit of conversation. They need someone who will listen while they describe their little aches and pains or listen to their reveries about the past. They want someone to be interested in all the little stories about their children or their grandchildren.

Sometimes people are so hungry for someone who will listen that they will tell their life history to the first stranger who shows the slightest sign of having a sympathetic ear. Just look around you, the next time you are in a train station, or a laundromat or a doctor's office, and you will see what I mean. There is an inherent need in every individual for communication.

Modern society recognizes the need and provides for it in many ways. Schools now provide counsellors to whom young people can tell their problems. Doctors and ministers usually have to spend a great deal of time just listening to people talk about their troubles. Business houses provide personnel managers so the workers can discuss their needs. Welfare workers must often be the "listening ear" for the poor and psychiatrists often earn their fees listening to the woes of the wealthy.

And yet, with all the provisions of our society and in spite of the huge masses of humanity with which most of us are surrounded day after day, the world is full of lonely people who are convinced that there is absolutely no one who cares or understands their deepest needs.

Thank God, there IS Someone who wants us to come to Him with our problems; Someone who ALWAYS has the time to listen; One who really and truly understands and cares. Better still, this dear Friend has the power to do for us according to our needs. It is His deepest joy to fulfill our every heart's desire.

Need someone to talk to? Then come quickly to Jesus! "For we have not an high priest which cannot be touched with the feeling of our infir- mities; but was in all points tempted like as we are, yet without sin. Let us therefore come boldly unto the throne of grace, that we may obtain mercy, and find grace to help in time of need" (Heb. 4:15, 16).

TELL IT TO JESUS ALONE

"Are you weary, are you heavy hearted?
  Tell it to Jesus, Tell it to Jesus;
Are you grieving over joys departed?
  Tell it to Jesus alone.

"Do the tears flow down your cheeks unbidden?
  Tell it to Jesus, Tell it to Jesus;
Have you sins that to men's eyes are hidden?
  Tell it to Jesus alone.

"Do you fear the gath'ring clouds of sorrow?
  Tell it to Jesus, Tell it to Jesus;
Are you anxious what shall be tomorrow?
  Tell it to Jesus alone.

"Are you troubled at the thought of dying?
  Tell it to Jesus, Tell it to Jesus;
For Christ's coming Kingdom are you sighing?
  Tell it to Jesus alone."

The Good Old Summertime

Summertime is here again!

Wonderful, wonderful summertime--with children playing in the sun...hamburgers grilled on an open fire...time to read and to play...a garden full of melons and squash and tomatoes...a chance to visit strange places...a time to visit neighbors and friends. After a long, cold winter, the prospects of summer seem marvelous indeed.

Or is summer a curse? Can it be that we will waste these three precious months by neglecting God's house, living for our own pleasure, and generally falling into a backslidden condition?

How pastors dread the summer months! Attendance often drops in Sunday School and church services and people forget the importance of prayer meeting. Somehow church members feel free to drop off the responsibilities of being at choir rehearsals, faithfully visiting absent Sunday School pupils, and carrying their financial end of the load.

Don't, DON'T let the summer be a curse to you! The time is too precious. Perhaps a suggestion or two would help.

1. Don't let the summer ruin your SERVICE. Be extra faithful with the Lord's work. Get busy in a vacation Bible school or volunteer to help for a week or two at a good Christian camp where boys and girls are being saved. If you must be away from your own church on a Sunday, then find a good church where the Gospel is preached and try to be a blessing there. This is a wonderful time to contact unsaved people and to get to know new families moving into your area. People are outdoors more and there are more opportunities for across-the-fence visiting. Summertime is soul-winning time.

2. Don't let the summer ruin your TESTIMONY. The warm days and the leisure time always present a temptation to Christian people to live just like the world does. Make certain you don't embarrass your pastor and grieve the Holy Spirit by what you wear in the summertime (or should I say, by what you don't wear?). Let your recreation and the places you do it be the kind that would glorify the Lord.

Your family life, with the open doors and out-door living of summertime, will be more exposed to your neighbors' view. Make sure that what they see and hear will honor the Name you represent.

3. Don't let the summer ruin your CHILDREN. How easy it is in the summertime to let children run wild. Mothers who are conscientious about the hours their children keep in the wintertime, sometimes do not even know where their children are in the summer. Don't neglect family devotions; your children need them now more than ever. Give your children something to do. Regular jobs and responsibilities in the home will do lots toward keeping your young people out of trouble. Encourage them to help in the work of the church too--cleaning, painting, mimeographing, taking care of the nursery during vacation Bible school.

4. Don't let the summer ruin your MIND. If you love to read, don't waste the summer filling your mind with trash. Spend extra time memorizing parts of the Bible and reading good books. This is a good time to read aloud to children. (Our little ones are currently very excited about missionary stories--they especially enjoy hearing anything about the life of David Livingstone.)

I hope your summer will be a blessing, not a curse!

Are You Patriotic?

The Fourth of July is over.

As usual, the city parks and forest preserves of the nation have been littered with the refuse of a million riotous picnics in "honor" of the day--soiled paper plates, cigarette butts, beer cans--haunting memories of degradation and lost virtue.

The highways have been littered too--with the rubber of a thousand skidding tires, broken glass and twisted steel and the carnage of human lives--haunting memories of carelessness, drunken revelry, and screaming sirens.

The hospitals have a few new patients; the jails have a few new inmates. There are a few more broken hearts and broken lives because we have once again celebrated the Fourth of July.

Here and there some people tried to remember what the day was all about. They planned speeches and erected memorials and sang "The Star Spangled Banner." There were brass bands and flags and fireworks and men in uniforms.

Somewhere, perhaps, a few even remembered to thank God for the heritage of liberty. Maybe somebody took a minute or two to be grateful for the rights which were desecrated so casually on this, our national birthday.

Christians should, of course, make the very best citizens, and the most patriotic. In the first place, our country was founded by God-fearing men who wrote its laws and outlined its responsibilities by the standards of the Bible. It goes almost without saying that a Christian ought to pay his taxes, uphold his government and vote, conscientiously and regularly. But these things alone do not fulfill our patriotic obligations.

When the Bible is replaced by atheism and evolution in the public schools of America, then Christians ought to speak out. When biblical scenes are forbidden in public places at Christmastime and Easter, then Christians ought to be heard protesting. Patriotism is not always merely "getting along nicely with one's neighbors." Sometimes patriotism means taking an unpopular stand in local and national issues. It might mean embarrassment for our children in schools and misunderstanding by our friends. We have failed our civic and moral responsibility at every point where socialism has gained a foothold in our national affairs.

A patriotic Christian has a duty to pray for our government and for all those in places of authority. God's Word has commanded us to do so (I Tim. 2:1, 2). We need the earnestness of Nehemiah who wept as he prayed for his country and his people:

"Let thine ear now be attentive, and thine eyes open that thou mayest hear the prayer of thy servant, which I pray before thee now, day and night, for the children of Israel thy servants, and confess the sins of the children of Israel, which we have sinned against thee: both I and my father's house have sinned."--Neh. 1:6.

Especially important is the kind of Christian patriotism which makes good citizens out of our children. May God give us perseverance and courage to teach our young people a fear of God, respect for law and authority, joy in learning to work hard and take responsibility.

If we accomplish this, then we may indeed call ourselves Christian patriots.

What kind of citizen are you?

Waste Baskets and Garbage Cans

I hope it is not an unusual characteristic of my children that they love wastebaskets.

Somehow they find it so exciting to rummage around and find old envelopes and discarded advertising circulars. When the mail comes they all stand around and wait to see what I will throw away. Colored advertising folders and window envelopes are the most sought after but they will gladly accept mimeographed forms or letters if nothing else is available. If I don't check up pretty often I discover that they have collected huge piles of trash which have been all tucked away in their drawers among their socks and pajamas and underclothes.

And how they love to collect small bottles and empty spools and cereal boxes! Bottles and boxes are so much fun for playing house or grocery store; spools are nice for making giant beads or doll furniture or barrels to be loaded on toy trucks. Small paper bags are just right for storing one's own private "things" and

discarded bits of aluminum foil make many wonderful things.

The outside is full of "treasures" too. Old bottle caps, rusty nails, gravel, and small sticks are often added to the collections I discover in the dresser drawers of my children. And I wouldn't dream of putting a pair of overall or a small dress in the wash without first examining the pockets. Experience has proved that to be absolutely imperative!

Baby Mark is even less fussy about what comes out of the garbage can. At the tender age of seven months he can already wheel his walker into position where he can get at all the "goodies" hidden in the garbage--leftover food, old apple cores, chicken bones, and bright pieces of paper. How hard it is for him to understand why Mommy says such a sharp "no" just when he is finding such interesting things to investigate! And how disappointed he is when all those delightful treasures are put up on the counter out of reach!

Of course my children are still pretty small. I keep hoping that as they grow a little older they will be a little more particular in their tastes. I hope they will eventually learn what

is valuable and what is worthless. And especially I hope they will learn the difference between temporary values and eternal values.

America is a nation of garbage eaters. Our
young people feast on moral rot in the movie
theaters and through the television screens.
The books available on every public newsstand,
the pictures in our magazines, the music that
fills our homes at the turn of a radio dial--all
offer us the vilest kind of trash imaginable.
The sad thing is that we have developed a taste
for that which is slightly rotten, slightly spoiled. We have forgotten how wonderful the good
and wholesome things really are.

We don't like to have our babies eating out of
the garbage can. I wonder--are we just as
particular about the mental trash cans out of
which our young people are eating? Are we
ourselves tasting the leftovers from the Devil's
garbage can?

"Finally, brethren, whatsoever things are
true, whatsoever things are honest, whatsoever things are just, whatsoever things are
pure, whatsoever things are lovely, whatsoever things are of good report; if there be any
virtue, and if there be any praise, think on
these things."--Phil. 4:8.

Stains! Stains! Stains!

How do little boys do it?

From head to toe, day after day, my boys come in covered with dirt and stains of all descriptions--grass stains, grease, rust, cookie crumbs and food stains, and of course a great deal of ordinary garden-variety mud!

Last night as I stood at the kitchen sink pouring quantities of bleach on a nearly hopeless little T-shirt, my husband suggested that some manufacturer of children's clothes just might make a fortune by producing little boys' shirts in mottled shades of black, brown and gray.

No matter what the advertisers say about their soaps and detergents, my laundry never comes out perfectly white and gleaming like the pictures portray. Even my bleaching and soaking is not the perfect answer--soon the colors begin to fade and tiny holes begin to appear where some little garment has been bleached just once too often.

Unfortunately, the rest of my house often shows the ravages of small hands and small feet. No matter how firmly I insist that hands must be washed after every meal, I nearly always find little finger marks about two feet high all along the bedroom hall! And the carpets and upholstery fare little better. How fast the grease spots and soil-marks begin to appear when there are children in the house!

Stains are a universal problem. Not merely the physical stains that defy our "wonder" soaps, but the stains on our consciences and our hearts that refuse to be cleansed by all our philanthropy and our good deeds.

I am always moved by Shakespeare's poignant scene of Lady MacBeth walking in her sleep, frantically trying to rub off the blood stains of guilt she sees on her hands after the murder of King Duncan. In her agony she sobs, "Out, damned spot! out, I say! . . . What, will these hands ne'er be clean?"

In Jesus' day, the Pharisees were fanatically careful about their ceremonial hand-washing, and yet the Lord said of them, "Now do ye Pharisees make clean the outside of the cup and the platter; but your inward part is full of ravening and wickedness" (Luke 11:39).

Pilate hoped to wash away his responsibility

223

for the death of Jesus with a little water. Matthew 27:24 says, "When Pilate saw that he could prevail nothing, but that rather a tumult was made, he took water, and washed his hands before the multitude, saying, I am innocent of the blood of this just person: see ye to it." But that little ritual did nothing to erase his part of guilt in the death of the Son of God.

How terrible are the stains of sin? But how blessed to know that there is a cleaning agent, better than any detergent, better than any hot water, better than any bleach--"... the blood of Jesus Christ his Son cleanseth us from all sin" (I John 1:7).

Do you ever go to bed at night heartsick at all the day's failures; disgusted with your own weaknesses and sins? Are you tired of all the dirty laundry of your life that just will not come clean, no matter how hard you scrub at it with good intentions and new resolves?

Then bring it all to Jesus. Whatever He washes comes out whiter than the snow! And here is the best part of all--when Jesus washes something He forgets that it was ever dirty. God sees us clean and pure--robed in the righteousness of His own Son. Just listen to the precious promise:

"I will forgive their iniquity, and I will remember their sin no more" (Jer. 31:34).

Well, I may never be able to remove all the stains from my home and my clothes, but I certainly do not need to keep the stains of sin!

The Roarin' Elgin

In our town they have been dismantling the old, defunct Chicago, Aurora and Elgin Railroad which used to carry all the suburban commuters and shoppers into Chicago. After operating in the red for a number of years the company was finally allowed to file bankruptcy proceedings and to go out of business. The men who used to rush to the station to catch the 7:55 a.m. "cannonball" for a swaying, jerky ride in a hot, smoke-filled car, now hurry to get a seat on an air-conditioned, double-deck Northwestern Railway train. The early commuters who were used to getting a quick cup of coffee at the station lunch counter (which always smelled like stale tobacco, fried eggs and disinfectant) now stop at Tom's Eat Shop, or some other local eating place.

It is true that old "Roarin' Elgin" did nothing to enhance our town from the standpoint of beauty. The garish red and blue wooden cars (replaced by slightly more modern ones in the last few years of its life) clattered past faded red and blue substations. The electric third rail was a danger and a menace to small children and to dogs who sometimes wandered near.

But still I am sad to see the empty gravel roadbeds where the tracks used to be, and the weeds now growing tall around the station platform. I miss the shrillness of the whistle, the clatter of the wheels. Most of all, I miss the symbol of excitement and adventure that train meant to me when I was a small girl. Every ride meant something special to see or to do in the Big City--shopping in a huge department store for a new coat, perhaps, or hearing a concert at Orchestra Hall or the thrill of visiting the Museum of Science and Industry. In those days, the 25-mile length of those tracks from Wheaton to Chicago might as well have encompassed the globe. I thought I had seen everything there was to see and done everything exciting there was to do when I had been to Chicago.

Well, the old Chicago, Aurora and Elgin Railroad is gone. Its cars have been sold or junked. Its stations are empty and silent.

No matter how much we resist them, changes

come into every person's life. The places we considered important once lose their significance once we've seen wider horizons. The possessions we once considered precious wear out or change or lose their appeal. The friendships we once cherished sometimes dissolve in disappointment and heartache. And death occasionally takes those who are nearest and dearest to us. Experience teaches us that life is not a comfortable little existence without change.

For a Christian change of circumstance ought to bring a change of values as well. It is not surprising that a starry-eyed youth will dream of worlds he hopes to conquer; the success he hopes to achieve in business or in service to mankind, the friends he hopes to make, the fame he hopes to acquire. But for a mature man (or woman) every physical loss, every disappointment in people, every failure of plans ought to be a reminder that life at its best is a vapor, changing constantly and soon gone. Nothing, absolutely nothing we can do or possess will be worth the snap of a finger unless it can be carried through the gates of eternity. How important it is, then, that we learn to value

those things which are not affected by the changes of this life.

". . . For what is your life? It is even a vapour, that appeareth for a little time, and then vanisheth away . . . . Be patient therefore, brethren, unto the coming of the Lord. Behold, the husbandman waiteth for the precious fruit of the earth, and hath long patience for it, until he receive the early and latter rain. Be ye also patient; stablish your hearts: for the coming of the Lord draweth nigh." --James 4:14; 5:7, 8.

What Are Mothers Made of?

Doesn't it take a lot of parts to make a mother?

For instance, a mother has to have a special kind of ears--ears that can hear the tiniest whimper of a baby in the dark of night; ears that can keep track of little children while they play; sympathetic ears to listen to the woes and joys of a teenager needing to talk.

And then a mother needs a special kind of eyes--eyes that are quick to notice the dirt behind a little girl's ears and the wiggle of a frog hidden in a little boy's pocket. A mother has to be able to read the heart's need of a child with her eyes--anxiety, deceit, frustration, disappointment. Most important, a mother has to have eyes that can see beneath the freckles and dirt and strawberry jam and see the potential of the preacher or missionary or Christian stateman who will change the course of history.

A good mother has to have special knees, too ...knees that do lots of bending--so that she can get low enough to play at building block

houses or give horsey-back rides or wipe up spilled milk. She especially requires knees that spend a great deal of time bent in prayer.

Feet are mighty necessary to a mother as well. How much walking a mother has to do--from stove to sink to refrigerator to crib to high chair to garbage can to broom closet to washing machine to clothesline--with paths crossing and recrossing a dozen times a day. A mother's feet have to be the kind that keep on going no matter how much they ache.

A mother has to have the right kind of hands --the kind familiar with the feel of soapy hot water and cookie dough and the handle of a broom. She needs hands that are tender when they bandage a cut finger, gentle when they wipe away a tear, skillful when they patch a pair of pants and firm when a little child needs to be spanked.

How wonderful it is that God gave mothers laps! A mother needs a lap where a child can bring broken toys that need to be fixed, books just waiting to be read and the many precious treasures which a little child might find in an afternoon of play. A mother needs a lap where a little child is always welcome when he is tired or hurt or unhappy or sick or just in need of a little love and she needs a lap where a child can find restoration and forgiveness after he has been punished for his sin.

But the best mother with all her attributes and gifts is only an imperfect picture of what God offers to His dear children who come to Him in need. His ears, more keen than any human ears, are always open to our cries of distress. His eyes see us, not clothed in the dirty rags of sin, but pure and holy, robed in the righteousness of His dear Son. His knees are never too mighty to stoop and bend to meet our most insignificant need. His feet can encompass the world in a single step to prepare the way and direct the lives of His own. His hands can hold the sun in its course or change death into life when it is in the best interest of His beloved children.

Best of all our Heavenly Father has a lap where we may bring all the broken toys of our lives for Him to fix--our unfulfilled dreams, our plans gone all awry. His lap is always waiting for us when we are tired or hurt or unhappy or just in the need of love. And when we have sinned and have felt the sting of His

rebuke, His lap is waiting where we may run for restoration and forgiveness.

"As one whom his mother comforteth, so will I comfort you."--Isa. 66:13.

". . .him that cometh to me I will in no wise cast out."--John 6:37a.

Mark Takes a Walk

Yesterday Mark took his first walk.

Little Mark is only eight months old and so he held tightly to Mommy's hand on one side and Daddy's on the other. But after weeks of covering his own little world inch by inch in a walker, he was eager to try out his own feet. He plunged down the walk with the perseverance of a Columbus and the courage of a Daniel Boone. The expression on his face was ex- quisite--such a glow of anticipation; such a breathless expectation of adventure! He was delighted with the florescence of the green grass in the morning sunlight and he had to stop and taste one long slender blade.

How many things there were to see and taste and feel--the colored gravel by the walk, the tiny clover blossoms, the cocky robin, the busy ant. What fun he had blinking at the sun and trying to catch the wind in his fat little hands! Every wobbly step was pure, pure pleasure; every new discovery was welcomed with a chortle of delight.

Watching Mark, I was suddenly aware of my own sated, disgruntled heart. How much joy I miss because I am blind to the beautiful wrappings with which the Lord surrounds every job He gives me to do; the bonus gifts of hands and eyes and feelings to enjoy the "good and perfect" gifts which we accept without a great deal of gratitude.

Worn out with the constant interruptions of little children, tired of the sameness of the household routine and bored with the lack of stimulating contacts with many different people day by day, housewives sometimes begin to feel that life is uninteresting and ordinary housework a drudgery. It is not unusual to find a young mother who, overwhelmed with the responsibilities of the household, feels unhappy and "put upon." The home for which she has longed and dreamed becomes a prison. The lovely wedding gifts--the linens, the dishes, become bothersome necessities that have to be washed and washed again. There is no joy in the preparation of a good meal; no pleasure in the crisp neatness of a freshly made bed or a newly scrubbed kitchen floor.

In the middle of a busy, trying day, it is

good to stop and "see" again with the joyful expectancy of a little child, all the blessings with which our loving Father surrounds us. It is a serious thing when boredom and self-pity are allowed to take root in the heart and grow into a tree of bitterness which branches out into every area of the spirit. Not only is the disposition spoiled but one's service for the Lord is often hindered as well.

Tomorrow let's enjoy the world like Baby Mark does. Thank God for every pleasant thing He gives to grace your home--the warm suds in your dishpan, the comfort of your favorite chair, the roof that provides cool shade in summer and warm protection in the winter, and especially the sweet round faces of children which are yours to wash and to kiss.

". . . His mercies fail not; They are new every morning; great is thy faithfulness."
--Lam. 3:22,23.

Every Little Girl Should Have an Aunt

Do you remember, as a child, some one person who was everything you someday hoped to be?

My little girl Carol has an aunt (really a great aunt) who is just such a person. Aunt Minner wears pretty dresses and shoes and she always smells like a flower garden. She has big wonderful purses full of exciting little boxes and pouches and tubes. Whenever children are at her house for breakfast, she makes little cardamon buns shaped like bunny rabbits and she never fusses if milk happens to get spilled on her pretty tablecloth. Aunt Minner lets little girls try on her jewelry and wear her perfume. When she bakes, she always takes the time to let little fingers pat the dough and shake the flour sifter. She never seems too busy to read story books or have a tea party. Aunt Minner enjoys taking little girls shopping and she even lets them decide what would be good to buy for lunch! If she gets tired of hearing children's songs and children's conversation, she never says so. "Best of all," Carol says, "Aunt Minner treats me like people--not like children!"

Every little girl should have an aunt. An aunt is a comfortable and familiar person, like Mommy, but since she doesn't often have the responsibility for administering discipline, that gives her a special quality.

I'm not a bit jealous of Carol's affection for her Aunt Minner because I know how often she reminds my children that their parents are "wonderful" or "smart" or "sweet." And frankly, I think Aunt Minner is rather a special person myself. Muriel (Mrs. Ray) Sandberg has some of those qualities I long for most. She always has a quiet trust in the Lord, and infinite patience. But of all her sweet Christian virtues, I admire most the fact that she always takes time for people--not just a few choice friends or loved ones but hundreds of people for whom others never seem to care. She and her husband, Ray, (who shares in this ministry of thoughtfulness) do all the sort of things that the rest of us wish we would do but never accomplish. I have seen them in hospitals and old peoples' homes, taking the time to visit strangers just because they seemed especially lonely or discouraged. They send out birthday cards each month to dozens of people who would not be in a position to return the kindness. They take special delight in surprising sick people and old people with candy or flowers. When they hear of someone in special need, they nearly always find some way to be of help.

It is a wonderful thing to take time for people. Jesus, busy with the greatest, most important mission of all the ages, took time for people. Though He could have spent His time brilliantly discoursing with the most learned and cultural men of His day, He spent His time with ordinary people--little children, fishermen, outcasts of society, crowd-followers. On at least one occasion He rejected the fellowship of His own family in order to be with those who needed Him most. And when He talked with folks, He talked with them on their own level; He was interested in their needs and burdens.

Aunts are wonderful people--especially the kind of aunts that take time for little people and lonely people and people in need. But all of us

could have the same ministry if we only cared enough.

"Then shall the righteous answer him, saying, Lord, when saw we thee an hungred, and fed thee? or thirsty, and gave thee drink? When saw we thee a stranger, and took thee in? or naked, and clothed thee? Or when saw we thee sick, or in prison, and came unto thee? And the King shall answer and say unto them, Verily I say unto you, Inasmuch as ye have done it unto one of the least of these my brethren, ye have done it unto me." --Matt. 25:37-40.